booksonline

Read this book online today:

With SAP PRESS BooksOnline we offer you online access to knowledge from the leading SAP experts. Whether you use it as a beneficial supplement or as an alternative to the printed book, with SAP PRESS BooksOnline you can:

- Access your book anywhere, at any time. All you need is an Internet connection.
- Perform full text searches on your book and on the entire SAP PRESS library.
- Build your own personalized SAP library.

The SAP PRESS customer advantage:

Register this book today at *www.sap-press.com* and obtain exclusive free trial access to its online version. If you like it (and we think you will), you can choose to purchase permanent, unrestricted access to the online edition at a very special price!

Here's how to get started:

1. Visit *www.sap-press.com.*
2. Click on the link for SAP PRESS BooksOnline and login (or create an account).
3. Enter your free trial license key, shown below in the corner of the page.
4. Try out your online book with full, unrestricted access for a limited time!

Your personal free trial **license key** for this online book is: 4a78-zq93-2wjm-drbe

Conception and Installation of System Monitoring Using the SAP® Solution Manager

Corina Weidmann, Lars Teuber

Conception and Installation of System Monitoring Using the SAP® Solution Manager

Bonn • Boston

Galileo Press is named after the Italian physicist, mathematician and philosopher Galileo Galilei (1564–1642). He is known as one of the founders of modern science and an advocate of our contemporary, heliocentric worldview. His words *Eppur si muove* (And yet it moves) have become legendary. The Galileo Press logo depicts Jupiter orbited by the four Galilean moons, which were discovered by Galileo in 1610.

Editor Florian Zimniak
English Edition Editor Justin Lowry
Translation Lemoine International, Inc., Salt Lake City, UT
Copyeditor Michael Beady
Cover Design Jill Winitzer
Photo Credit Fotolia/Anand Baid
Layout Design Vera Brauner
Production Editor Kelly O'Callaghan
Typesetting Publishers' Design and Production Services, Inc.
Printed and bound in Canada

ISBN 978-1-59229-308-7

2nd edition, updated and revised, 2010; 1st reprint, with corrections, 2011

1st German edition published 2009 by Galileo Press, Bonn, Germany

Contents

Introduction

The profitability, capability for innovation, and competitiveness of an enterprise depends on how fast and efficiently it can adapt its processes to changes in the market. There are three types of processes:

- **Business processes that run in the business**
  These are processes concerned with the core business of the enterprise, that is, the business processes that are largely responsible for the success of the enterprise.
- **Processes that represent the basis for a stable, smooth flow of the business processes**
  These types of processes originate from information technology (IT). They are called the operative IT processes.
- **Cross-area processes between business and IT**
  An example is the application support processes. Cross-area processes require communication and coordination between the business and IT areas.

As this short description already suggests, "processes" is a topic that requires a lot of attention and must be checked at regular intervals. These checks are usually implemented by the process manager via a permanent monitoring of the process flows.

Now, you would think that constant monitoring of the processes is enough, but that's not the case. Process monitoring alone doesn't guarantee a stable, smooth, and system-controlled process flow. On the one hand, individual process areas cannot be 100% autonomous; they are interdependent in many cases. On the other hand, processes are often operated to support application software. This software requires hardware with various system components, and these system components and the entire IT infrastructure must be monitored just as the processes themselves are. The IT components form their basis and are as important for the functioning of an enterprise as the processes.

Over the last several years, system landscapes have become more complex due to the use of innovative system components. These system components are not only

SAP® systems, but also applications outside of SAP. For the IT staff of an enterprise this means that they are constantly learning how to administer and monitor these different system environments. Most of the time, the responsibility of these systems, and the training of staff, lies in the hands of a small number of employees — because not everyone can be an expert in every departmental area. This means that knowledge is decentrally organized.

With regard to system monitoring, you can safely state that an expert does a very good job in his specific area of expertise, which means that, due to the decentralized organization of the specialist areas within the IT department, there is a high degree of quality and, at the same time, a high expenditure of time for system monitoring. This expenditure can be reduced by automating and centralizing the monitoring process of heterogeneous system landscapes, which should be the objective of any enterprise.

The implementation of automated system monitoring must be handled like a project. Experience has shown that customers believe that the implementation of system monitoring and the associated alert management does not require a lot of time. This is true when it comes to the implementation itself. Before the implementation, however, there is the design phase; only then can you integrate automated system monitoring and the setup of an alert management within a live operation. Be aware that the increasing complexity of the system landscape requires automation and time for the implementation. Therefore, it is very important to specify the components of the systems that must be monitored and which alarms must be handled in which way. Not every monitoring object is useful and necessary.

In the first edition of this book, the necessity for central monitoring was already discussed. The experience that we've gained since then shows that many enterprises have already recognized the necessity for implementing monitoring despite a limited number of staff or a tight IT budget. Now the question is which tool supports automated monitoring and can be used for all tasks throughout the whole operation, for example, in an IT support department that documents its messages in a ticket system. The answer to this question will not surprise you: SAP Solution Manager.

With this new edition we want to update you on the latest developments with SAP Solution Manager 7.0, and provide you with information about central system monitoring using this powerful application management tool.

Contents of this Book

In this book you will find information to facilitate the conceptual design and implementation of a centralized system monitoring. You will get an overview of the aspects you should consider in the design phase of your monitoring system, followed by the implementation, which is supported by the use of SAP Solution Manager.

To get away from pure theory, a sample scenario runs throughout this book. This sample scenario describes the system landscape of Toys Inc., a fictitious enterprise. Based on the initial situation of this enterprise you will see, step-by-step, a decentralized system monitoring process converted into a centralized one.

Target Audience

This book addresses readers who manage and monitor both SAP and non-SAP systems; those who are currently on the lookout for an appropriate monitoring tool for their own system landscape are also invited to take a look at the following chapters. And perhaps you will find yourself in a situation where you have to implement a centralized system monitoring process and can use this book as the basis for selecting relevant monitoring objects.

Prerequisites

To fully understand the contents of this book you should have experience in the administration of SAP and non-SAP system components. You should be familiar with the specific SAP terminology and that of other related areas. And, finally, it will prove advantageous if you have knowledge of the SAP monitoring architecture *Computing Center Management System* (CCMS).

Contents of the Individual Chapters

Chapter 1, The Problem and a Sample Scenario, describes why centralized system monitoring has advantages over a decentralized approach. Apart from this, we will introduce SAP Solution Manager as a monitoring tool and explain which requirements must be fulfilled to successfully implement centralized monitoring. In this context you will also find information on the design of a monitoring concept. As already mentioned, we will refer to Toys Inc., whose initial system monitoring concept will be described here.

Chapter 2, SAP Solution Manager, provides you with a comprehensive overview of the functionality of SAP Solution Manager. We will describe various possibilities of how to integrate and use SAP Solution Manager in your system landscape, and introduce the SAP Solution Manager as an implementation platform, a solution monitoring platform, a service provider platform, a service channel to SAP Service Marketplace, a documentation platform, and a service desk platform.

Before you set up system monitoring within SAP Solution Manager you should consider which system components and modules to include in the monitoring process. These considerations are discussed in **Chapter 3**, Designing the Monitoring Concepts, which deals with the creation of a monitoring concept. The monitoring concept includes select monitoring objects, such as system availability and SAP buffer settings.

In **Chapter 4**, System Monitoring Using SAP Solution Manager 7.0, you will learn how system monitoring can be configured and mapped for a specific system landscape in SAP Solution Manager. Various screen captures will guide you through the SAP Solution Manager. And to give you a practical and concrete overview of the functional scope regarding system monitoring, we will demonstrate navigation with the fictitious system landscape of our sample enterprise, Toys Inc. SAP Solution Manager Release 7.0 will serve as the basis when we set up the system monitoring. All of the menu paths and names specified here refer to this release. Please note that in other releases the interface and navigation paths might not correspond to those in Release 7.0.

Chapter 5, IT Performance Reporting, describes how to set up and use the Business Warehouse (BW) performance reporting. This last chapter describes how to activate BW reporting in the SAP Solution Manager system to make IT performance reporting available.

1 The Problem and a Sample Scenario

In this chapter we lay the foundation for the monitoring concept used throughout this book. We discuss the advantages of centralized over decentralized monitoring, describe the basic functions of SAP Solution Manager, and outline a sample scenario for our concept.

1.1 Centralized and Decentralized System Monitoring

The following criteria show you what should be considered when you decide to implement centralized or decentralized system monitoring. The list is not exhaustive so you should consider it a guide to ask yourself which kind of monitoring is best suited for your enterprise.

- **Efficiency**
  Time and efficiency depend on each other. Every enterprise strives to use the capacity of its employees in such a way that there is a balanced relationship between the utility of their activities and the underlying effort. Suppose a highly qualified information technology (IT) administrator spends most of his working hours monitoring systems, which is important for a smooth system operation, but for the enterprise, this is not efficient at all. So, if you consider all of the specialists in the IT department who are responsible for system monitoring, it is much better to centrally bundle the working time that each individual spends on monitoring his specific area.
- **Technical expertise**
  An employee who specializes in a certain area of expertise for which he is responsible in a decentralized model would probably achieve better results in this area than a person who monitors the entire system landscape. However, such knowledge and expertise can be integrated in a centralized monitoring concept that focuses only on the essential aspects of system monitoring. In this case you define a certain number of monitoring objects and threshold values. That is to say, based on your own experience, you specify the values that tell

you when a problem is about to occur within a system or when you have to act to ensure continued system operation.

- **Single Point of Access**
  Suppose someone asks you:
  - which systems you monitor?
  - where most of the system problems occur?
  - what is the current release of the systems in use?
  - which SAP and non-SAP systems are you currently using?
  - which parts of the systems you think could be optimized?
  - if you have adhered to the service level agreements with other business partners (for example, of the application) in the past five months?

  In a decentralized system monitoring model you can easily ask the relevant people to get an answer to all of these questions. But what would you do if someone wanted you to answer on the spot? Wouldn't it be much nicer to manage and monitor your system information as a whole? Or rather, wouldn't it be great to have just *one* point of access to all of the information you need?
- **Communication interfaces**
  Both decentralized and centralized system monitoring contain communication interfaces. In the centralized monitoring model, the number of interfaces can be higher than in the decentralized one because more people may be involved in the monitoring process. For example, there is an additional interface between the person who monitors the systems and the one he refers problems to. However, you should keep in mind that a high number of interfaces can affect total system performance.
- **Monitoring additional system components**
  In times like ours, where new software components and technologies enter the market ever more rapidly, the shape of a system landscape changes accordingly. To keep pace and to keep track of which system and application components are already or will be included in the system monitoring process, a centralized system monitoring model offers great benefits.

All of the preceding criteria support the implementation of a centralized model. Due to an efficient time management and a clear definition of tasks, centralized system monitoring enables you to minimize or even avoid negative financial effects for an enterprise after a failure of its IT systems. In this context, monitoring activities are automated and processes necessary for system monitoring and troubleshooting are defined.

So, IT specialists, such as a database expert, are able to concentrate on their core areas of expertise and study other areas at the same time. This gives workers the freedom to familiarize themselves with new technologies, which results in a further optimization of the stability and performance of your systems.

The centralized character of the monitoring process moves the collaboration of different application components in a heterogeneous system landscape into focus. No longer are individual system objects regarded as separate entities because it is much more important to see the interaction between these objects and to find out which interdependencies exist between them if the system fails at some point.

1.2 SAP Solution Manager

SAP Solution Manager is application lifecycle management software developed by SAP. It forms the central platform in a solution landscape and the business processes of your enterprise.

SAP Solution Manager provides the appropriate tools, for example, in Change Management, to support you in the implementation of *IT Infrastructure Library* (ITIL) processes. These processes are described, documented, configured, and tested. The processes are monitored when they go live, and they must be optimized and adapted as required.

SAP Solution Manager provides a central access to a pool of tools, methods, and preconfigured contents that offers support during both the implementation and the operation of your SAP system landscape.

1.2.1 Implementation

SAP Solution Manager supports you during the entire lifecycle of your solutions (see Figure 1.1). You can perform implementation projects and upgrades of SAP solutions by using centralized information and project management.

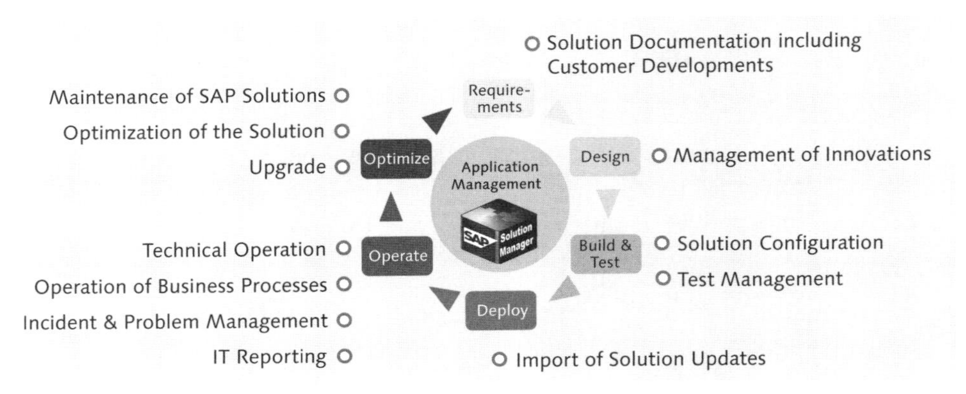

Figure 1.1 SAP Solution Manager as the Central Platform in the Lifecycle of a Solution Landscape

In other words, as early as the introduction of new solutions, SAP Solution Manager provides you with an implementation platform. This platform provides *methods* and *tools*, based on Best Practices, to which you have centralized access during the complete period of implementation — from the business blueprint to the final implementation. All of the steps necessary for the implementation of a solution are arranged in roadmaps, and centralized storage of project documentation within SAP Solution Manager enables you to quickly access all of your project information.

In addition, SAP Solution Manager provides you with extensive knowledge gathered by consultants and support staff over the course of customer projects.

Predefined project phases are also available to you, which are supposed to facilitate the implementation of business processes. For example, if you want to integrate a Supply Chain Management (SCM) system or another SAP Business Suite solution into your system landscape, you will find predefined process and configuration descriptions in SAP Solution Manager to do this.

SAP Solution Manager also contains documentation that is needed for your system landscape. This means that when you run both an ERP system and an SCM system, documentation for these components is automatically provided in SAP Solution Manager. Documentation can be Best Practices, for example, that focus on one specific subject within an SAP component, such as how liveCache Backup and Recovery is necessary to run an SCM system. These documents are prepared by experienced SAP support employees and must be adapted in accordance with specific customer requirements, if required.

Apart from the functions already described, SAP Solution Manager also provides so-called *roadmaps*. A roadmap is a guideline for an implementation project. You learn step by step what you have to consider during an implementation and in which order the steps are to be carried out.

Another important tool that compares the customizing objects of a system in an SAP system landscape with customizing objects in SAP ERP is *Customizing Synchronization*. For example, you can compare the customizing of an SAP SCM with that of the SAP ERP system. You should use this tool to avoid differing customizing settings in individual SAP components. By comparing the settings or the specific customizing objects with each other you can keep them in sync.

After the implementation of a new solution and the new functions that go with it the users have to be trained. You can use *E-Learning* in SAP Solution Manager to create learning maps from existing project structures. These learning maps are available to users at any time and contain an overview of the functions a user needs to perform his tasks within the new system solution.

The *test management* of an implemented solution after specific project phases is an essential part of every project. You can organize and perform tests at certain project stages by using the Test Organizer. To do this, you create test plans or test packages for individual testers in SAP Solution Manager, and information on the progress of such tests can be retrieved at any time.

And if you plan to upgrade one or more SAP components, then *Upgrade Project Management* in SAP Solution Manager can help you. This tool contains all upgrade activities and it transparently documents all changes you make in your SAP components.

1.2.2 Operations

In addition to the tools already mentioned, SAP Solution Manager provides specific functions for the operation of a system landscape.

In the solution-monitoring area you are provided with a centralized system administration and system monitoring in real time. You not only monitor the systems, but also adapt the business processes to the individual requirements of the enterprise.

In SAP Solution Manager, solution monitoring consists of three monitoring areas:

- **Business Process Monitoring/Interface Monitoring**
  Here the focus is on real-time monitoring of business processes. Business process monitoring focuses on alarms related to the technical operation of a business process, such as the performance of a transaction or the monitoring of interfaces.
- **System Monitoring**
  The focal points of system monitoring are the centralized system administration and the real-time monitoring of all system components relevant to business processes.
- **Service Level Management (SLM) and EarlyWatch Alert (EWA)**
  SLM is used to check if agreements with and objectives of business partners are adhered to. You can check such agreements and objectives by using the *Service Level Reporting* function in SAP Solution Manager. Service Level Reporting is based on the data collection of SAP EWA. SAP EWA is a monitoring tool that monitors certain administrative areas of SAP components, compares them with reference values, and evaluates accordingly. It runs automatically, for example, once a week, and informs you about already-existing critical or imminent problems within your system.

The centralized system administration allows for uniform access to the solution landscape, your system configuration, and the handling of all tasks associated with system administration. These tasks can be defined and provided with time specifications. If the date expires and the task has not been confirmed by the administrator responsible, you receive a notification about the administration task. Depending on the SAP components you use, the preconfigured, component-specific administration tasks are scheduled. The Landscape Reporting function then enables you to retrieve information on your system landscape from a central location in SAP Solution Manager whenever you want.

Another function is the integrated *Service Desk,* which provides the possibility of efficient message processing. In the *Support Desk* area, SAP provides you with the Incident and Problem Management functions that are necessary for service and support. Service Desk is an integral part of SAP Solution Manager 7.0. In particular, you can map the ITIL processes Incident, Problem, and Change Management.

And with *Notes* you can even build a solution database. Depending on the respective product, you link non-SAP ticket systems via a standard interface. This function is frequently used within the scope of certification audits, for example, SAS 70, which is is an audit standard published by the American Institute of Certified Public Accountants. With this audit, service organizations, such as application service providers or data centers, want to obtain a confirmation that their enterprise has a functioning, internal control system for IT processes. An enterprise that is subject to the Sarbanes-Oxley Act (SOX) must provide this certification.

One of the greatest challenges in IT is to ensure high availability. The use and the integration of different technologies within a solution landscape increase complexity and decrease clarity; therefore, it is even more important to use instruments that help you identify problems quickly and efficiently. For this reason, a new functionality was developed for SAP Solution Manager, the *Root Cause Analysis*. The goal of the Root Cause Analysis is to identify and localize problems in a solution landscape and take actions for the problem solution so that the work process of the end user is not affected.

1.2.3 Optimization

Optimization is the third and recurring part in the lifecycle of a solution.

SAP offers various *services* in the context of its support activities. These include the SAP EarlyWatch Check, SAP GoingLive Check, SAP Remote Performance Optimization, and SAP Solution Management Optimization Services. These services can be performed in SAP Solution Manager. With SAP Solution Manager you have a portal at your disposal that enables you to directly connect to the *SAP Service Marketplace* and *SAP Support*. SAP Solution Manager enables you to quickly and easily order services provided by SAP. For example, if there is a problem with your system's performance and you urgently need an analysis, you can send a service order from the SAP Solution Management Optimization program in SAP Solution Manager. The service can then be run within SAP Solution Manager. With the link to the SAP Service Marketplace you also have direct access to SAP Active Global Support and the SAP Notes provided via the SAP Solution Manager if there is a problem.

If you have to adapt your solution to new requirements, for example, by importing support packages; implementing SAP Notes; installing add-ons; or changing scenarios, processes, and individual process steps, you have to perform several steps before the change can be implemented in the target system. To do this, you can use *Change Request Management* and the Maintenance Optimizer in SAP Solution Manager. This tool enables you to perform changes within your solution with minimal risk and effort in terms of both financials and time spent. They optimize the control, monitoring, and retraceability of all software change processes.

Chapter 2, SAP Solution Manager, provides further information on the tools of SAP Solution Manager.

1.2.4 The SAP Solution Manager System Availability During Operation

The SAP Solution Manager system is a production system like any other. However, the requirements on the availability of the system strongly depend on the use of scenarios or functions in SAP Solution Manager. For example, if you use the *monitoring* scenario, you must ensure that the system is available in accordance with the requirements and that a solution is at hand in case of system failure. If you use it for documentation purposes, the high availability of the system is disproportionate to the necessary effort and the associated costs. The service and support processes that are supported by SAP Solution Manager are decisive for determining the required availability.

Each production system also entails a test or development system — this also applies to SAP Solution Manager. If a three-system landscape cannot be implemented for whatever reason, you at least need a system that functions as a test *and* development system in addition to the SAP Solution Manager production system. Changes to an SAP Solution Manager production system can be as critical as changes to any other production system.

The system requires the same administration work as any other system, including tasks such as the definition of maintenance times, creation and implementation of authorization concepts, definition and regular implementation of administration tasks, system monitoring, creation and implementation of a backup and recovery strategy, definition of IT processes, support activities, and so on.

You must be aware of the significance of the SAP Solution Manager system when you decide to use it as a central tool and the costs and effort this entails.

1.3 The "Monitoring" Project

At the beginning of a project, you have an idea: "Let's optimize the existing monitoring system and create a central and possibly fully automatic monitoring and alarm generation."

Once the initial euphoria about the idea has calmed down, actions need to follow. The idea becomes a project, or in this case, it is the *system monitoring* project.

Today, the implementation of central monitoring must not be done along the way. Even if only individual components are added, they must be considered holistically and in the context of the whole system. But reality is usually different, and the amount of work is often underestimated, which can lead to discouragement among the employees if the idea doesn't become a success or wrong priorities are set. Therefore, an idea with serious intentions should turn into a project to achieve the desired success.

1.3.1 Project Management

A project is a plan that pursues a specific goal in a coordinated manner — be it the solution to existing problems or the implementation of specifications or ideas. By means of project management you use methods and tools that support the implementation of the project. To run the project in the terms of the project management, you must define basic conditions and expectations, such as content, scope, chances of success, budget, time, staff, and so on.

Each project is divided into multiple project phases. Initially, an analysis is carried out, with the goal of identifying weak points that can have a significant influence on the enterprise. In the design phase, you define the conceptual design, and create a concept based on the requirements you added in the analysis phase—you design your "product," so to speak. Next, you implement the concept, which is followed by the test phase. The monitoring process is carried out during all phases with regard to cost control, adherence to schedules, project progress, and so on.

If you apply classic project management to our monitoring project, the rough project flow could look as shown in Figure 1.2.

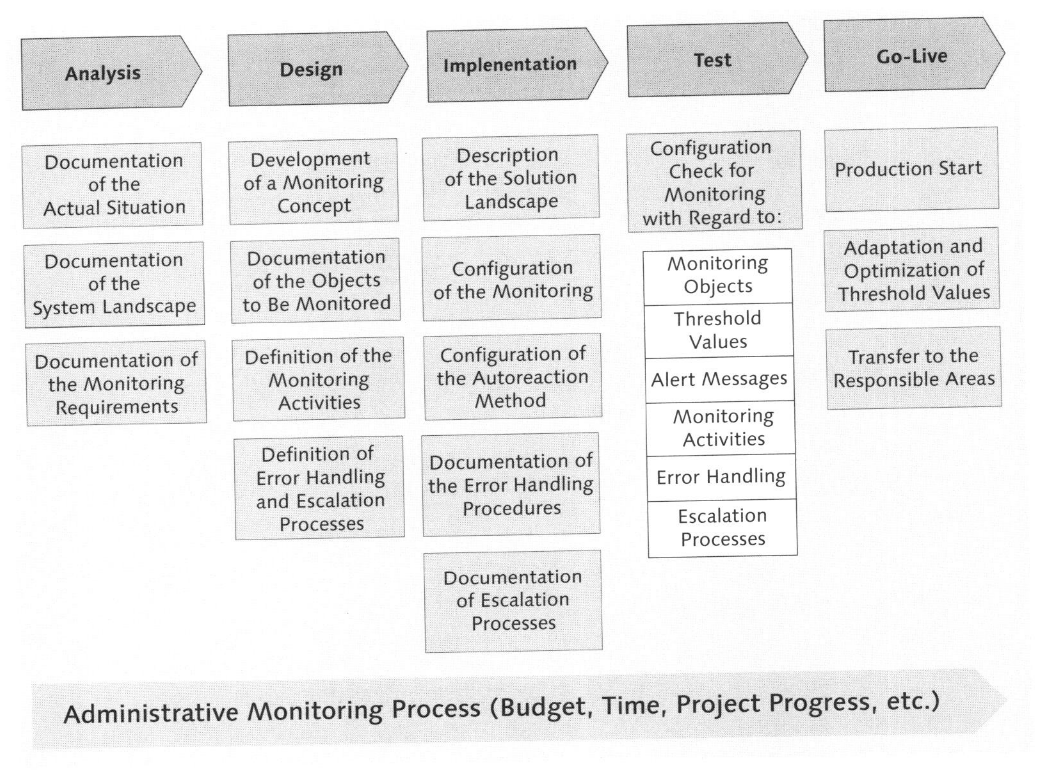

Figure 1.2 Example of a Project for the Implementation of System Monitoring

Because this book focuses on the design and implementation of system monitoring in the SAP Solution Manager, we will not go into further detail about the project work itself and the additional activities needed for its successful completion.

1.3.2 Monitoring Concept

Basically, it doesn't matter which monitoring software you use for centralized system monitoring. The best tool is useless if you don't document the requirements for centralized monitoring before the configuration and implementation of the monitoring application starts. This simply means that the implementation of a monitoring system needs to be prepared accurately. Following the common project approach, the conceptual design of monitoring is developed based on requirement and weak-point analysis. This conceptual design specifies:

- who the person in charge of system monitoring is
- who takes responsibility for which particular area
- the specific requirements for system monitoring
- which system components to monitor
- which monitoring objects to include in the system monitoring solution
- how frequently the monitoring objects have to be monitored
- the suitable threshold values
- when an automatic notification is sent if a threshold value is exceeded
- who the automatic notification is sent to
- what the necessary procedures are in the case of an escalation
- what monitoring software to use
- how reporting is structured

Keep in mind that the creation of a monitoring concept takes some time. The more detailed the requirements of your centralized system monitoring solution, the easier it will be to decide which monitoring components to include in the monitoring process. And besides, don't forget that a monitoring concept can just be the basis for all other things that follow. Once it has been implemented and you start gathering your own experience in centralized monitoring you can refine your concept constantly.

Chapter 3, Designing the Monitoring Concepts, provides information on the elements you should include in your monitoring concept.

1.3.3 Project Team

Regardless of the scope of a project, such as the implementation of centralized system monitoring using monitoring software, you have to build a project team. In doing so, you should consider the following two options: Either build a project team to concentrate exclusively on the design and implementation of the centralized monitoring solution, or build a team that does the project work along with its everyday work.

In terms of quality, it is better to have a dedicated project team for the design and implementation of a centralized monitoring solution that is relieved of its daily tasks.

But apart from quality, time is also important. A dedicated project team can finish its job in a shorter timeframe, which would result in an earlier implementation and go-live of the centralized monitoring solution.

To conclude this section, here are some tips to help you build up your project team:

- **Identify a project lead**
  The project lead is responsible for both the design and implementation of the monitoring concept. The project lead should have an overview of the entire scenario because he assumes the coordination role of the project.
- **Identify the project members**
  When you select the team members make sure that every one of them contributes their individual knowledge about system monitoring to the concept. You should include employees who can define the key performance indicators (KPIs) and who have experience with monitoring tools.

1.4 Toys Inc.: Initial Situation

To clarify why the creation of a monitoring concept and a concept for implementing centralized system monitoring in SAP Solution Manager is important, we'll use the system landscape of a fictitious enterprise, Toys Inc., as an example.

1.4.1 Enterprise

With its headquarters in the U.S., Toys Inc. is a medium-sized business that produces plastic toys. The enterprise has three locations worldwide: the U.S., Germany, and Singapore. In each of these locations there are two production sites and two distribution centers. The enterprise's peak season begins in August and ends in December. In the low season (January through July) production takes place 12 hours on weekdays while during the peak season (August through December) there's 24/7 production. Both the suppliers (e.g., for materials) and the customers are spread around the globe.

1.4.2 System Landscape

To support the sales, production, and distribution of its products the enterprise uses ERP Central Component (ECC) system 6.0, while requirements planning and production planning are carried out with SAP SCM 5.0. A warehouse management system is used to manage the warehouse stocks. For the two SAP systems, a development, testing, and production system is available.

The portal with SAP NetWeaver 7.0 is used for the enterprise's Web presentation. Customers can send their orders directly from there. An enterprise-internal intranet is also implemented using the SAP NetWeaver Portal system, which is separated from the other systems and the development system through an additional firewall for security reasons.

An SAP NetWeaver Business Warehouse (BW) system is used for mapping statistics for internal decisions and planning, and a development and testing system is available for the BW system.

The SAP Solution Manager system forms the platform of the solution operation and consists of a production system and an additional, combined testing and development system (see Figure 1.3).

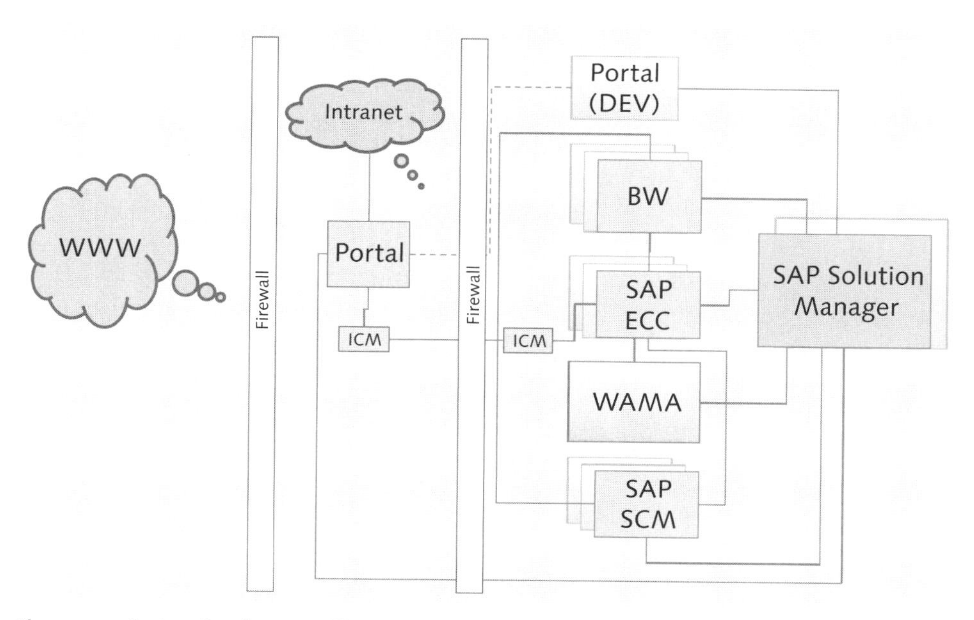

Figure 1.3 System Landscape at Toys Inc.

1.4.3 IT Department

Due to restructuring measures, the IT department was reorganized. Management focused on cost reduction and higher efficiency of the IT area.

The systems are serviced from the U.S. because the entire IT department is located there. The IT department consists of four main groups — the basis team, application management, system administration, and IT support (see Figure 1.4). Within these teams there is a further separation of responsibilities according to different areas of expertise. The Service Operations IT area is superordinate to the other four groups.

- **Basis**
  The basis team maintains the systems with regard to databases and operating systems. This work involves tasks such as installation and administration. Some members of the basis team are responsible for the creation of data backups that might be needed in the case of a system recovery. The hardware management includes the procurement and maintenance of new hardware, whereas the network administrators have to maintain the entire networking landscape. The security management group provides protection against external influences, such as unwanted external access to the systems. Both the monitoring of the individual areas and the handling of problems within the base area is ensured by the team.
- **Application management**
  The application management team maintains the entire application — from the commissioning to the operation to the further development of the application. It supports system administration with performance problems and is responsible for the smooth operation of the applications. This includes the monitoring, maintenance, and optimization of the applications. The application management team is responsible for users and the assignment of authorizations, and the application development and document management. An expert is available for each subject area to analyze problems and provide solutions using different methods and tools.

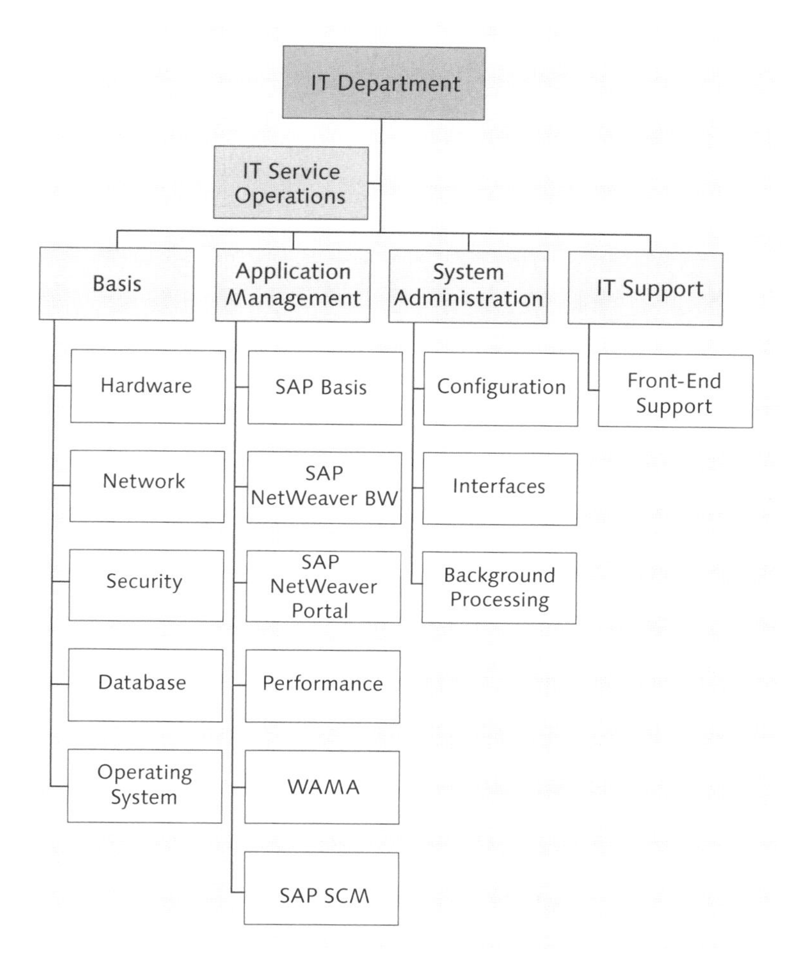

Figure 1.4 Organization Chart of the IT Operations Department at Toys Inc.

- **System administration**
  The system administration team does nothing else but ensure the smooth operation of applications. Here, the focus is on up-to-date applications and the implementation of recommendations from the application management team. Part of this team's responsibility is to enable good system performance, which involves the proper maintenance of basic system settings, such as the buffer settings. Interfaces, like the *Core Interface* (CIF) between an SCM system and an ECC system, are monitored by both the technical support and the application.

The most important aspect about background processing is that the systems are able to process all background jobs planned within a certain timeframe without reaching their resource or performance limits.

- **IT support**
  The IT support team maintains frontend PCs. For example, if a user has a problem with a PC, this team handles the troubleshooting.

- **IT service operations**
  The IT service operations area has multiple functions. It is the link between the business and the IT department. This forms a communication platform for two large departments of the enterprise. The goal is to ensure more cooperation and to implement innovations or changes as efficiently as possible. In addition, this area creates, integrates, and controls IT services that exist between the two groups. For example, an IT service can monitor an application to ensure that a solution is provided in case of an alarm.

1.4.4 System Monitoring

Each member of the four teams has to perform various tasks. And one of these tasks is the monitoring of the systems. When doing this, every employee concentrates on part of the system he specializes in by using the tools available to them in their individual system areas.

For example, the database expert is responsible for the smooth operation of the databases in all systems. One of his jobs is the management of existing datasets, which means that he must know where to find individual datasets and check the database growth within certain periods.

An expert from the application management team checks system performance on a regular basis. That is to say, from time to time, he has to find out if the response time of the systems is still acceptable. And yet another person monitors the resource utilization of the machines, such as memory and CPU utilization.

From a professional point of view, this decentralized type of monitoring provides the best results in terms of quality because every one of these employees can make a reliable judgment and tell how critical or noncritical an upcoming problem might be for the running system operation. However, all employees have the same problem: nobody has an overview of the entire system landscape. There is no central point of contact that only takes care of the monitoring of all system components. The fact that nobody has a complete overview of the system landscape means that it is impossible for an individual team member to find out whether there are problems in different locations of the system that could be related to each other.

1.4.5 Problems with the Existing System Monitoring Process

As a result of the existing monitoring system and a glance back into the past of the monitoring process, the following problems have emerged:

1. **Response time — system availability**
   One of the main problems at Toys Inc. is the long response time in terms of problem recognition, particularly with regard to system availability. There is no plan to use a high-availability solution. Therefore, the downtime of a system can only be reduced by responding quickly to system failures. The reduction of the response time is supposed to minimize the system downtime to almost zero, especially from August through December, with the necessary but plannable maintenance not being included in this calculation.
2. **SAP buffer settings**
   In the past, the SAP buffer settings were often the cause of performance problems. It is therefore reasonable to include the SAP buffers into the centralized system monitoring process.
3. **Job monitoring**
   Another problem is the monitoring of background jobs that have to run regularly for technical reasons. These are maintenance jobs that are regularly planned because they are necessary to achieve a smooth system operation. One of these jobs is the SAPconnect sending job that typically runs every ten minutes and checks if there is new email in the queue and, if so, sends it directly from the queue. If this job doesn't run you cannot send any email from an SAP system.
4. **Database accesses — database time**
   The SAP system landscape at Toys Inc. contains a large number of proprietary developments. And in the past there have often been problems with database access times, which were caused by long-running SQL commands in the proprietary applications. This in turn led to longer database response times and hence to performance bottlenecks. In the future, it is necessary to attach more importance to shorter database response times to avoid such problems altogether.

5. **Performance bottleneck in the portal**

   The enterprise has an Internet presence. This Internet presence enables customers to place orders. For some time now, customers have complained about performance, so the challenge for IT is to find the cause. The performance problem can have many causes, such as, the network could be affected, the processing on the server side in SAP NetWeaver Portal, or the problem could be caused by the memory system.

   Various solutions are possible here, but the right approach to identify the cause is complex because various areas must work together. A suitable tool has not been used so far.

1.4.6 Overcoming the System Monitoring Problems

To reduce their problems with system monitoring, or even avoid them altogether, Toys Inc. has decided to set up a project team. In this new project team, each team of the IT department is represented by one of its members.

The project team's objective is to optimize the monitoring of system components within the existing solution by carrying out structural changes in the IT department and implementing a monitoring tool.

On the basis of this objective the team has to perform the following activities:

- Set out the requirements for future system monitoring activities
- Define the quality criteria to be monitored
- Establish measures to eliminate existing system monitoring problems to meet future requirements
- Perform these measures within a reasonable timeframe.

2 SAP Solution Manager

SAP Solution Manager collects information about the applications contained in a system solution and the business processes run by these applications. It provides a central transparent data source that can serve as a basis for numerous decisions and activities in your IT organization. In addition, the central data collection ensures consistency of individual decisions and related activities.

Apart from the description of your solution landscape, SAP Solution Manager provides more comprehensive functions and scenarios to implement and operate your SAP solution. These are briefly explained in the following sections.

However, before the basic functions are described, first let's discusses the *work center* concept in SAP Solution Manager.

2.1 Work Centers

A work center is a defined working environment in SAP Solution Manager that centrally provides functions and relevant information that are related to certain responsibilities, for example, for the administration of the solution landscape.

There are different work centers for various scenarios in SAP Solution Manager. The following work centers are available:

- Business Process and Interface Monitoring
- Change Management
- Root Cause Analysis
- Implementation/Upgrade
- Incident Management
- Job Management
- System Landscape Management
- Setup
- System Administration
- System Monitoring

Work centers were first provided with Solution Manager 4.0 SP 15 and SP18 will add more work centers and optimize the existing ones.

You cannot access all of the work centers in the standard version. The corresponding authorizations are assigned with the respective work center role, but we won't discuss work center roles further because the SAP Solution Manager's Implementation Guide (IMG) provides more information on this topic.

Figure 2.1 shows the System Monitoring work center. From the setup of the monitoring to the evaluation of the collected monitoring data, all information is stored in the same work center.

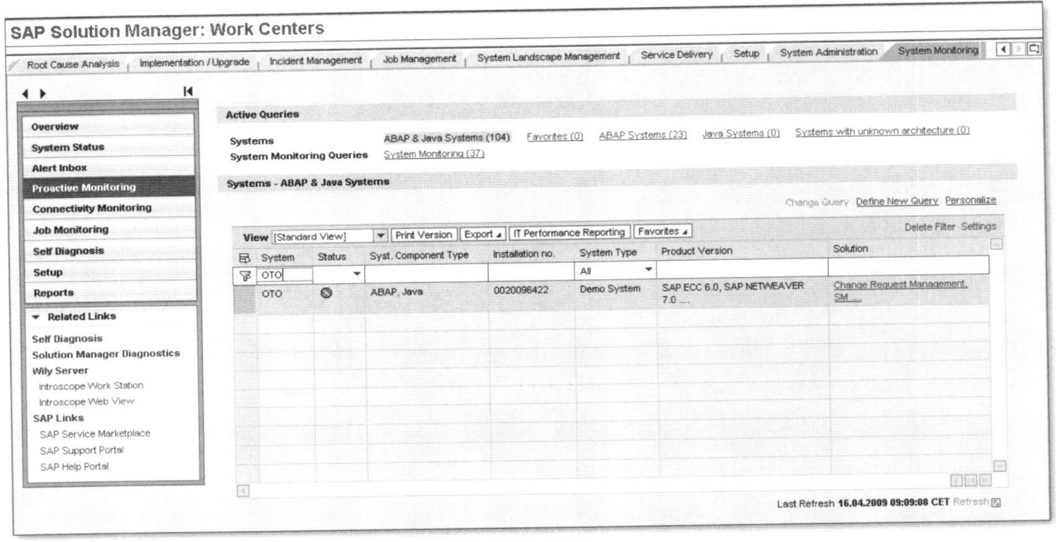

Figure 2.1 System Monitoring Work Center

2.2 Scenarios of SAP Solution Manager

SAP Solution Manager supports various system management scenarios during the lifecycle of a solution landscape, and it also supports the Run SAP methodology. This methodology enables you to implement an end-to-end solution operation, that is, a consistent application and business process management.

In the following sections we will analyze some of the scenarios in SAP Solution Manager.

2.2.1 Implementation and the Upgrade Platform

The integration of new SAP scenarios, such as SAP Supply Chain Management (SCM), SAP Supplier Relationship Management (SRM), or the very first implementation of an SAP product in a system landscape are carried out in the form of a project. Projects are process oriented, which means they do not focus on the implementation of just one component, but rather on the complete implementation of entire business processes so that cross-system processes are optimally supported as well. In this respect, you use the tools and utilities that are commonly used in project management.

An important project management tool is the use of separate project phases and their subprocesses. Thus, in terms of its progress, a typical project for the implementation of an SAP solution can look like the following:

1. Project preparation
2. Business blueprint
3. Implementation
4. Final operations
5. Go-live and support

SAP Solution Manager provides the option to centrally manage and run the entire project from the implementation phase through going live. Various tools and methods are available for this, and you can map all of the relevant components of a project in SAP Solution Manager (see Figure 2.2).

In SAP Solution Manager there are six different types of projects:

- **Implementation project**
  The implementation project (see Figure 2.2) is based on the selection of business processes. There are two options to perform an implementation project. Either you set up a process structure according to one or more already-existing templates or you decide to use your own process structure.
- **Optimization project**
  An optimization project is used to optimize the flow of business processes or as a software solution. As a support service, SAP provides defined standard services that you can carry out in SAP Solution Manager.

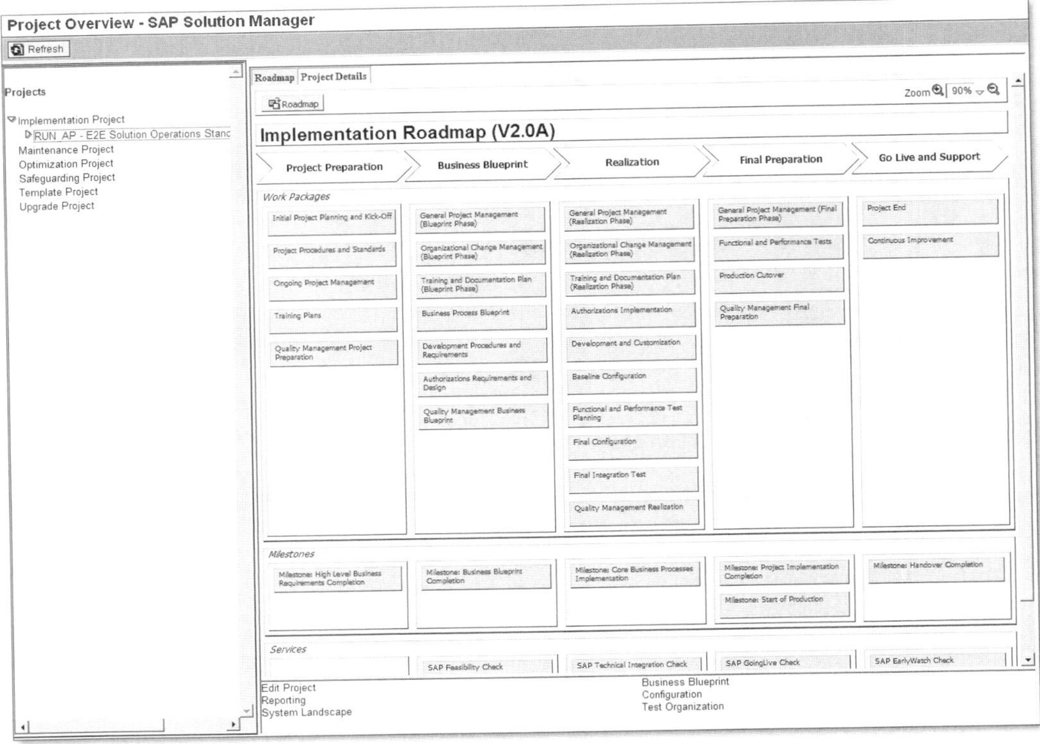

Figure 2.2 Global Project Overview in SAP Solution Manager 7.0

- **Safeguarding project**
  The safeguarding project is used if unexpected problems occur during the implementation or operation of an SAP solution. This project type supports you in organizing, coordinating, documenting, and resolving critical situations.
- **Upgrade project**
  The upgrade project enables you to identify and perform the necessary tasks to upgrade an SAP component.
- **Template project**
  The template project is used to create templates for other projects. The project structure of a template project can be used for any other project.

- **Maintenance project**
  The maintenance project supports you in managing change requests (Change Request Management). It maps all maintenance-relevant activities, from coordination to implementation.

2.2.2 Solution Monitoring

When you monitor a system landscape the most important aspect is to guarantee the smooth operation of all your systems. This means you must ensure the availability and performance of the systems. In this context, certain components of the systems or of the system landscape are checked at different planned intervals and used as a kind of "warning signal."

You can perform an automated or a manual monitoring of the system landscape. In either case you have to define Key Performance Indicators (KPIs), which serve as a basis for monitoring. Not only does the term KPI imply that the systems are dealt with regarding their performance; they are a large number of technical indicators that point to defined situations or changes of system states. This book uses the term KPI for all indicators — even though not all of them are performance indicators.

Threshold values have to be specified for the KPIs. The threshold values are defined in such a way that they trigger an alarm upon the detection of a problem. The alarm either indicates that a problem will soon occur within the system landscape (*proactive monitoring*) or that the system is already in danger and that action must be taken immediately (*reactive monitoring*).

System Monitoring

In its broadest sense the term *system monitoring* means the monitoring of technical components, which also includes the performance and availability of a system. For example, this includes the utilization of hardware resources, databases, system availability, system configuration, ERP Central Component (ECC) configuration, operating system (OS) parameters, SAP liveCache, SAP Business Connector (BC), SAP Internet Pricing Configurator (IPC), SAP Internet Transaction Server (ITS), and so on. The administrative section of the IT department is responsible for system monitoring.

Figure 2.3 gives you an overview of the system groups in SAP Solution Manager 7.0. It displays several SAP systems with their components, for example, the C50 system with the Customer Relationship Management (CRM) components.

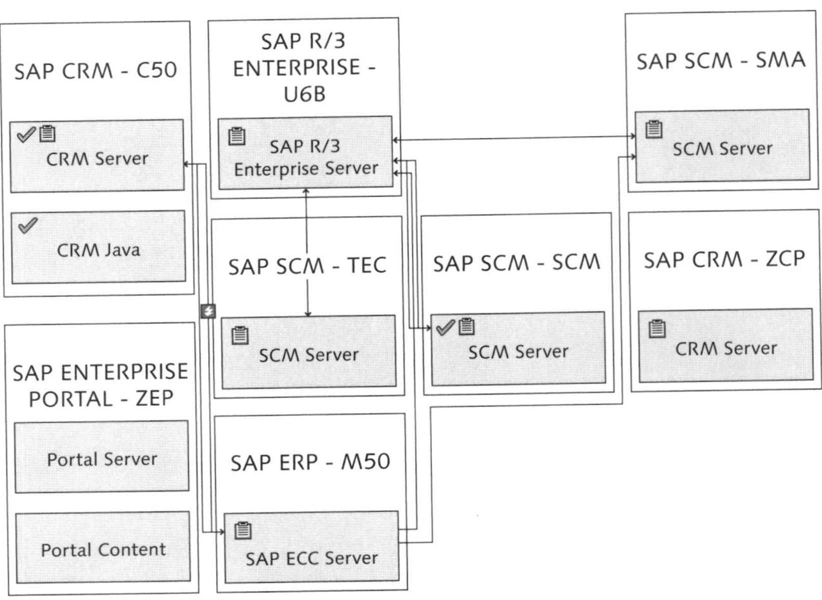

Figure 2.3 System Monitoring in SAP Solution Manager 7.0: System Group Overview

Business Process Monitoring

Monitoring critical business processes within an enterprise involves business process monitoring in an application. The main focus of this activity is the monitoring of business processes or individual process steps that can become critical for an enterprise if they fail to work properly. For example, it is possible to monitor background processing activities within a business process. In addition, SAP Solution Manager enables you to monitor the application logs of specific objects, such as the Application Link Enabling (ALE) log.

Every enterprise uses specific business processes. However, the majority of the processes are quite similar. Let's take the example of the creation of a quotation. Every enterprise has to create quotations. The difference here is how the quotation is created. In other words: Which internal approval workflow is defined, which responsibilities are given, which IT systems are used, and which documentations are required? This is the individual approach to a process in an enterprise. Moreover, every enterprise defines business processes differently. Either very detailed or one or two levels above. As an introduction to and for support of business process mapping in SAP Solution Manager, SAP Solution Manager provides business process templates for individual SAP components. You can retrieve them from the Business Process Repository. Now you have a basis for a process that you can adapt to your own process.

The following example illustrates the relationship between technical system monitoring and business process monitoring.

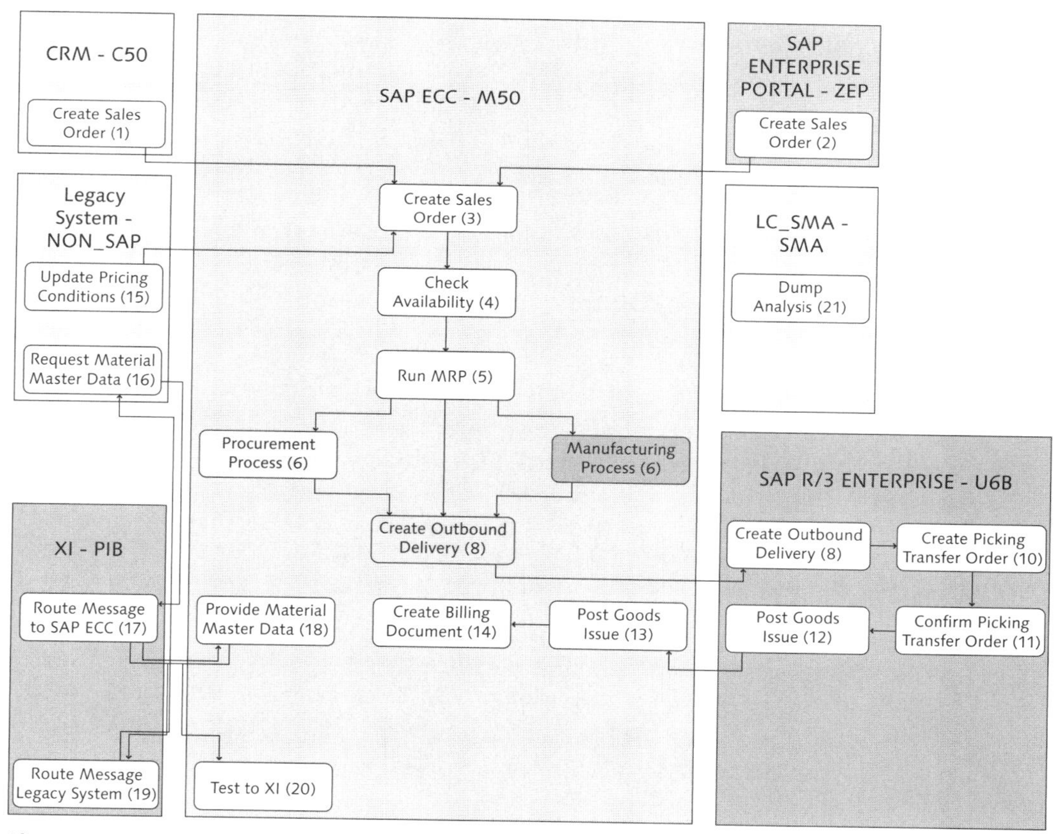

Figure 2.4 Example of Business Process Monitoring in SAP Solution Manager 7.0: Business Process "From Sales Order to Invoicing"

A business process includes everything from sales orders to invoicing as shown in Figure 2.4. Now the question is to what extent does this process affect the database? An I/O load is generated, which means that a specific table gets updated. How can you measure this process? The business process cannot really be measured, but you can specify various measurement criteria, for example, the number of updates. This means that, from a technical point of view, business processes are represented as data movements, CPU load, memory load, and so on. By measuring these technical details you can draw your conclusions regarding the business process. Thus, to monitor a process means to check its technical ramifications.

Interface Monitoring

Interface monitoring distinguishes between technical and application-oriented monitoring. Technical monitoring involves the monitoring of the entire network and the individual communication links within the system landscape. Application-oriented monitoring, on the other hand, focuses on the correct processing of jobs in the target system.

SAP Solution Manager enables you to monitor interfaces, such as transactional Remote Function Call (tRFC), queued Remote Function Call (qRFC), ALE, or Electronic Data Interchange (EDI) from both a technical and an application-oriented viewpoint.

If you want to perform application-oriented interface monitoring you should first map your business processes in the business process monitoring tool of SAP Solution Manager, otherwise it wouldn't make any sense (see Figure 2.4). This means:

1. You create a business process that substantially adds to the success of the enterprise. This business process is divided into business process steps. Each of these individual business process steps performs a task in a specific component environment. If the tasks are distributed across several systems, interfaces between these systems will emerge as a result. These specific interfaces have to be monitored. Figure 2.4 illustrates an interface between two business process steps — Update pricing conditions (15) from a non-SAP system into ECC to the Create sales order (3) process step.
2. Once the business process, including its individual steps, has been mapped in SAP Solution Manager you can begin to configure and set up the interface monitoring.

Figure 2.5 illustrates application-oriented interface monitoring between several business process steps. If you double-click on the interface symbol you can obtain detailed information about the interface. You can assume monitoring responsibility directly via the application support.

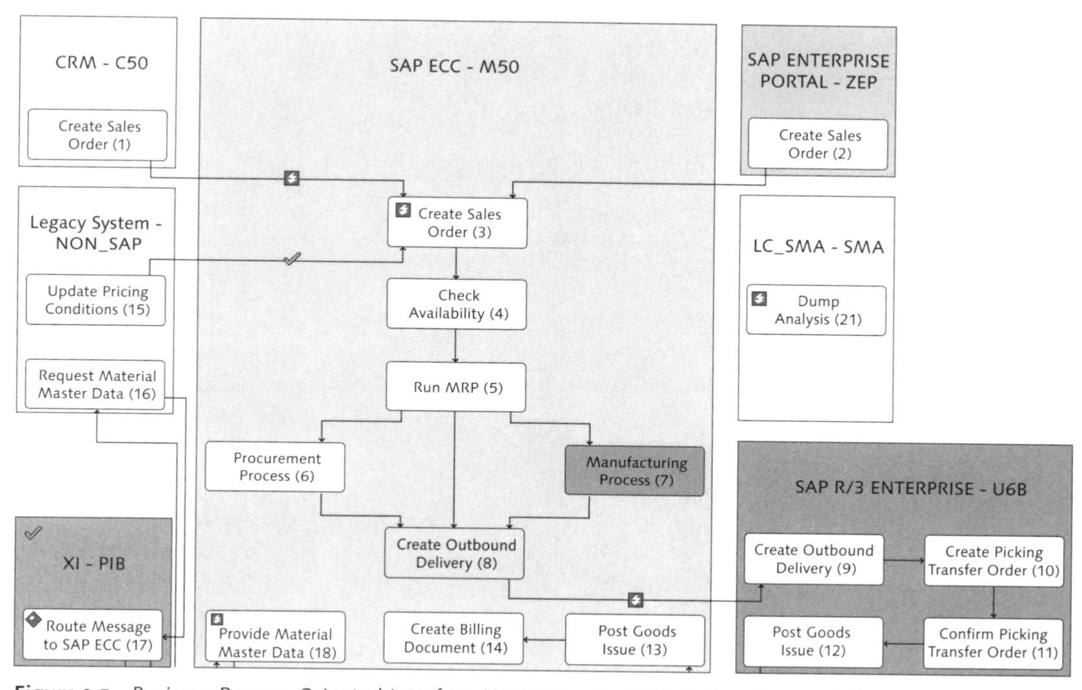

Figure 2.5 Business Process-Oriented Interface Monitoring in SAP Solution Manager 7.0

Figure 2.6 shows an example of technical interface monitoring. As previously mentioned, technical interface monitoring involves the monitoring of network components and individual communication links within the system landscape. To set up technical system monitoring you must first map your system landscape in SAP Solution Manager. However, in contrast to application-oriented interface monitoring you don't need to map the business processes.

Figure 2.6 illustrates multiple SAP systems and one non-SAP system. There is, for example, an interface from the C50 SAP CRM system to the M50 SAP CRM system. This interface will be included in the system monitoring process. You can obtain detailed information about it by double-clicking on the interface symbol.

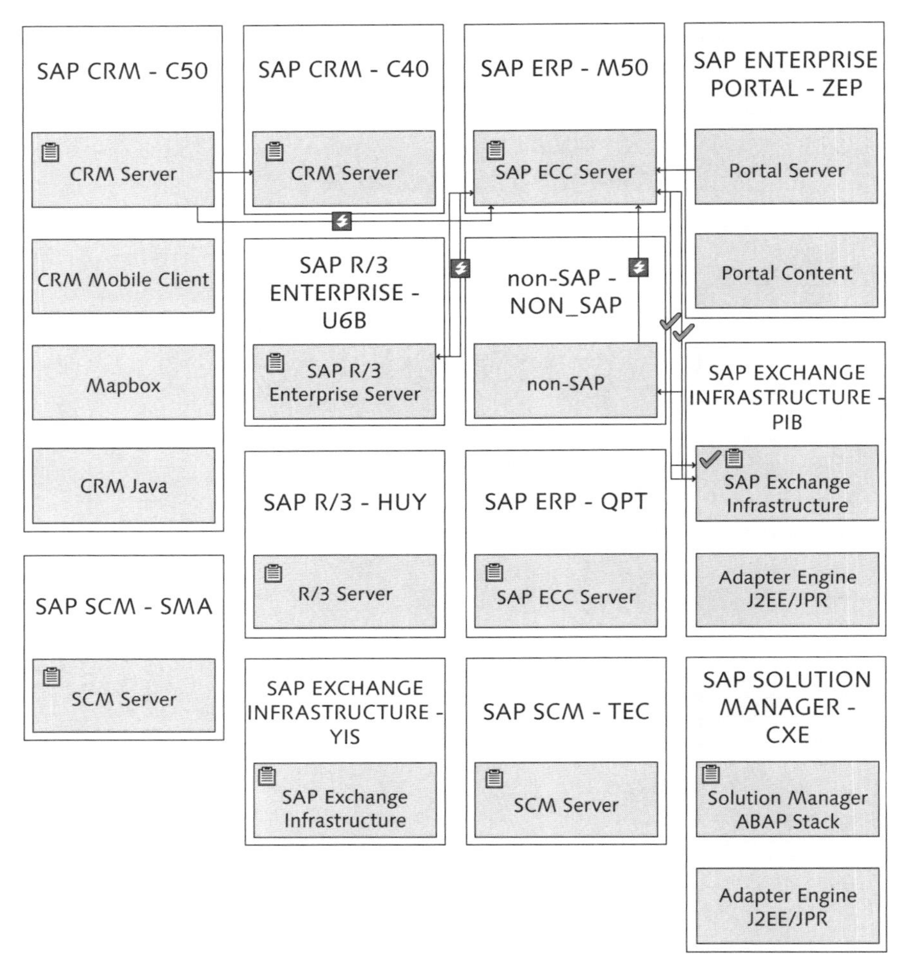

Figure 2.6 Technical Interface Monitoring Between Two SAP Systems in SAP Solution Manager 7.0

Service Level Management

You conduct *service level management* to check if agreements and objectives that have been arranged for with a business partner are adhered to. A business partner could be a hardware supplier, a software supplier, the implementation partner, the outsourcing partner, a customer, or a support organization.

The parties involved define requirements in the form of specific key performance indicators (KPIs), such as system availability times or the response time behavior of certain transactions. The identification and definition of such indicators are stipulated in so-called *Service Level Agreements* (SLAs). Service Level Reporting, in turn, generates the results and evaluations of the SLAs.

The goal of service level management is to achieve quality assurance in the long run that, due to improved communication, raises the level of satisfaction for both the IT organization and the users. This goal can be achieved by clearly defined objectives, instructions, budgets, and communication structures.

Service Level Reporting

Service Level Reporting serves to evaluate service level agreements upon which the IT organization and user have agreed. When doing this you can include factors from the business processes and indicators from the system landscape. But it is important that you know upfront what kind of information you want to integrate into the reporting process. Therefore, it is advisable to focus on a specific target audience. You may either need a summarized report for your managers or a rather detailed list of everything.

IT-related information, such as system and application data, is provided in all systems. The challenge is to select, evaluate, and map the most important data for the respective target group.

SAP Solution Manager provides two options in reporting. In addition to common service level reporting, you can also have the system display system and application information using SAP NetWeaver Business Warehouse (SAP NetWeaver BW). The data can be sent to an external BW system and displayed in the integrated BW system in SAP Solution Manager.

SAP EarlyWatch Alert

The SAP EarlyWatch Alert (EWA) is a proactive service by SAP and component of the reporting in SAP Solution Manager. It provides information about the state of individual systems and their applications within your SAP system landscape. Depending on the configuration, it can run daily, weekly, or monthly. It is recommended, though, to run the EWA report once a week.

Depending on the SAP solution you use (SCM, ERP, CRM, and so on), the SAP EarlyWatch Alert contains predefined default parameters such as ABAP Dump Statistics or statistics about transactions with the best response time behavior.

The SAP EWA is available for ABAP and Java systems. An EWA report is created for every SAP system and the corresponding components.

Figure 2.7 provides an overview of the SAP EWA in SAP Solution Manager.

Solution Monitoring | Service Desk | Change Management | Solution Reporting | Service Plan | Issue Management

EarlyWatch Alert | Service Level Reporting | System Monitoring / Administration | Business Process Monitoring

Create | Delete | Save Services | Show Archive Queue

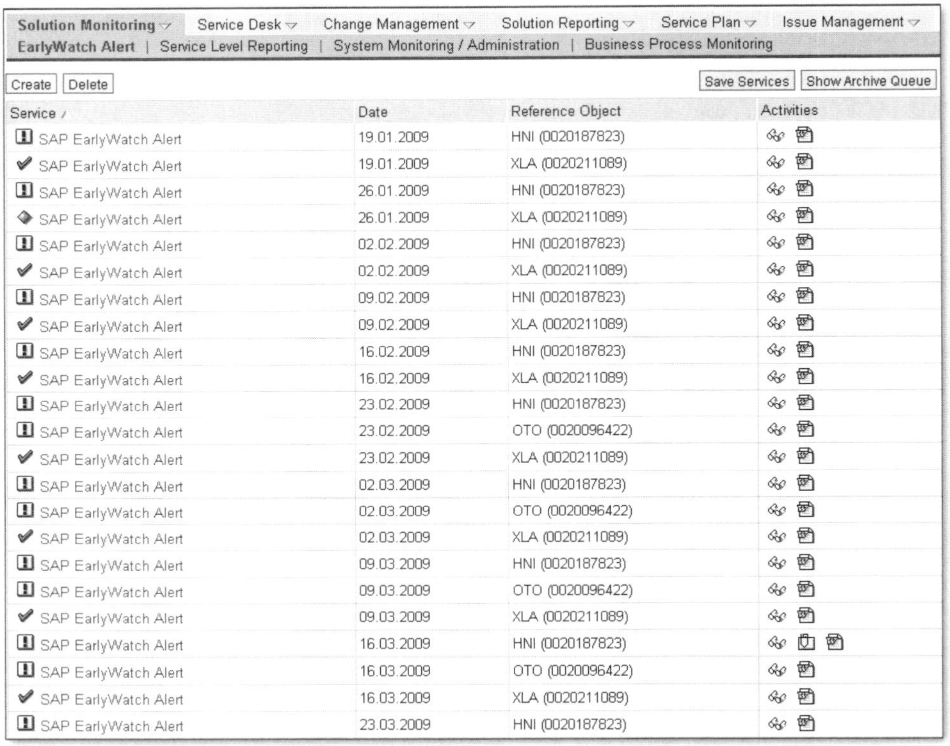

Service	Date	Reference Object	Activities
SAP EarlyWatch Alert	19.01.2009	HNI (0020187823)	
SAP EarlyWatch Alert	19.01.2009	XLA (0020211089)	
SAP EarlyWatch Alert	26.01.2009	HNI (0020187823)	
SAP EarlyWatch Alert	26.01.2009	XLA (0020211089)	
SAP EarlyWatch Alert	02.02.2009	HNI (0020187823)	
SAP EarlyWatch Alert	02.02.2009	XLA (0020211089)	
SAP EarlyWatch Alert	09.02.2009	HNI (0020187823)	
SAP EarlyWatch Alert	09.02.2009	XLA (0020211089)	
SAP EarlyWatch Alert	16.02.2009	HNI (0020187823)	
SAP EarlyWatch Alert	16.02.2009	XLA (0020211089)	
SAP EarlyWatch Alert	23.02.2009	HNI (0020187823)	
SAP EarlyWatch Alert	23.02.2009	OTO (0020096422)	
SAP EarlyWatch Alert	23.02.2009	XLA (0020211089)	
SAP EarlyWatch Alert	02.03.2009	HNI (0020187823)	
SAP EarlyWatch Alert	02.03.2009	OTO (0020096422)	
SAP EarlyWatch Alert	02.03.2009	XLA (0020211089)	
SAP EarlyWatch Alert	09.03.2009	HNI (0020187823)	
SAP EarlyWatch Alert	09.03.2009	OTO (0020096422)	
SAP EarlyWatch Alert	09.03.2009	XLA (0020211089)	
SAP EarlyWatch Alert	16.03.2009	HNI (0020187823)	
SAP EarlyWatch Alert	16.03.2009	OTO (0020096422)	
SAP EarlyWatch Alert	16.03.2009	XLA (0020211089)	
SAP EarlyWatch Alert	23.03.2009	HNI (0020187823)	

Figure 2.7 SAP EWA in SAP Solution Manager 7.0

2.2.3 Service Desk — Incident Management

Another scenario that you can map in the Service Desk of SAP Solution Manager is *incident management*. You use the Service Desk to centrally collect and manage all problem inquiries (called *incidents*) that arise in the applications or during the technical operation of the various systems in your system landscape.

You then have a complete overview of all messages. Due to the centralized nature of the Service Desk you can see:

- what types of messages have arrived
- what status they have
- how long they have had their current status
- which messages have been processed
- which messages have been completed
- if the response time regarding the level of priority for processing these messages has been observed

Figure 2.8 illustrates the centralized character of message processing in SAP Solution Manager. Your SAP Solution Manager is connected to all of your system components. Messages can be sent to SAP Solution Manager from each system component and, in turn, you can receive information about the processing status of a message. If necessary, you can forward a message to SAP for further processing. Messages that SAP has replied to are sent back to customer status within SAP Solution Manager.

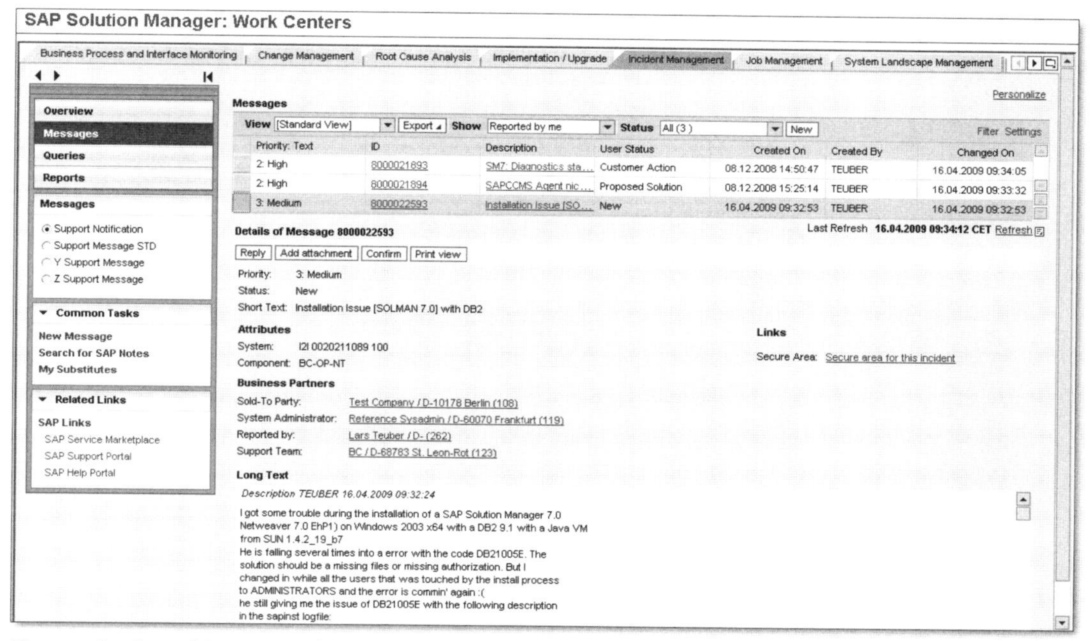

Figure 2.8 Central Support with the Incident Management Work Center

In the Service Desk you can map your own support organization. You can implement and set up your support organization in the Service Desk yourself or in cooperation with an SAP consultant. But to do this, you must know the organizational structure of the support (that is, the definitions of functions, roles, responsibilities, and service components), the support processes, and the SLA.

A standard support process could look as follows:

Initial situation: The user can no longer work in the SAP system and needs support.

Solution: The user opens a message in the SAP system he's currently using. In the HELP • ENTER SUPPORT MESSAGE menu he can create the message. He chooses the relevant component, enters a short text, and specifies a priority for the message after which he has to describe the problem. In addition, he can also send an attachment with the message, for example, information on an ABAP dump. When all of the information has been entered he can send the message to the Service Desk in SAP Solution Manager. In addition to the information entered by the user, the message also contains information about the system, for example, the OS and database versions, the support package level, and even the transaction the user is currently working in. That way, the person who processes the message doesn't have to search for this information in the system or obtain information about the sender from a different location. The amount of additional information greatly facilitates the processing of the message.

In the Service Desk you can automatically assign the message to the corresponding unit to a specific person within the support organization.

After receiving the message the support agent has two options: He can either provide a solution after receiving answers to possible questions from the sender; to find a solution, he can use the Solution Search in the solution database of the Service Desk and the integrated search for SAP Notes in the SAP Service Marketplace. Or the support agent forwards the message to another agent within the same support organization or directly to SAP Support. To forward messages to SAP, an interface to the SAP Global Support Backbone is available.

After forwarding the message to SAP, SAP Support will provide a solution to the problem. Every time the status of the message changes an automatic transfer occurs. In the SAP Solution Manager system you can specify how often the transfer has to occur.

2.2.4 Root Cause Analysis

Solution landscapes and the underlying technologies become more and more multifaceted. It becomes increasingly difficult to find the cause for IT problems, because multiple technologies are used in a system landscape. To identify the cause of a problem in a complex system landscape with different technologies, you need generic tools that support you.

Let's have a look at an example to illustrate the significance of the Root Cause Analysis:

Employees in a call center receive telephone orders every day. They enter sales orders via a portal system. The sales order itself is created in the connected ERP system. Previously, the ordering process took four minutes at the most. Now, it requires considerably more time. Employees and customers are dissatisfied.

Why does the ordering process take so long? What is the problem? Is it a network problem, a performance problem, a database problem, or...? Which system component is responsible for the delay in the ordering process?

To find the cause, a structured procedure is required. The top-down method and specific tools enable you to localize the problem. To do this, you can use the following SAP Solution Manager tools:

- Workload Analysis
- Trace Analysis
- Change Analysis
- Exception Analysis

The Workload Analysis provides an overview of the performance of your system landscape. By defining generic performance parameters and comparing the actual data, you can check to see if there actually is a performance problem. If so, you can use the component-specific analysis tools to analyze the problem.

The Trace Analysis is useful if a problem is caused by long-running user queries. In this case, the trace is activated and records all transactions and their response times during the processing of the data. Targeted checks of the individual transaction steps and the distribution of the response times help you localize the problem.

The Change Analysis provides you with an overview of all changes in the respective systems that have to be managed. The Change Analysis is required to check, for example, when the ABAP parameters were changed last so that you can clarify whether the change caused the problem.

The Exception Analysis is the central entry point for an analysis of functional problems in a solution landscape. This tool enables you to identify components that trigger an exception. However, why this component has triggered an exception must be analyzed with component-specific analysis tools. For example, in Java environments the Log Viewer is used, Transaction ST22 for analyzing ABAP runtime errors.

For more information on this topic, refer to *Performing End-to-End Root Cause Analysis Using SAP Solution Manager* by Michael Klöffer and Marc Thier (SAP PRESS, 2008). This book provides detailed information on analysis tools and their areas of use.

Figure 2.9 shows the Root Cause Analysis work center, which provides these tools.

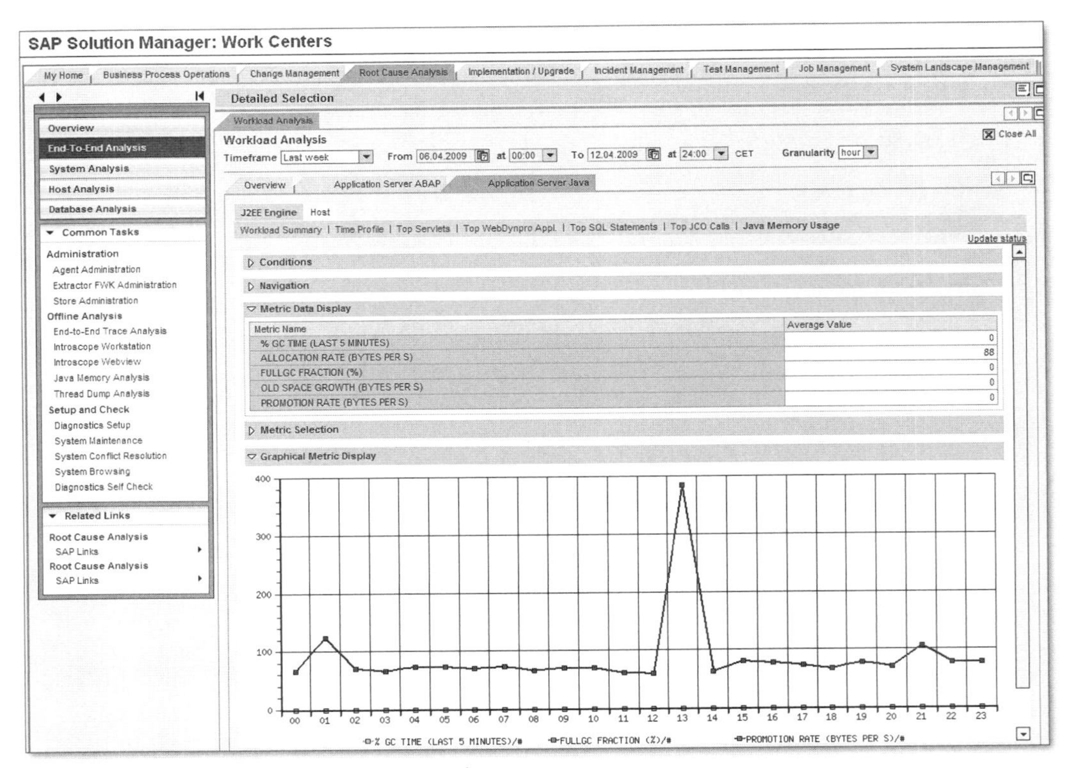

Figure 2.9 Root Cause Analysis Work Center

2.2.5 Change Request Management

Change Request Management in SAP Solution Manager enables you to process change requests and coordinate their implementation. Integration with Transport Management allows Change Request Management to control change requests from SAP Solution Manager centrally. Various change types are used here to meet the different requirements of the change processes. Additional functions, such as reporting or object locks, support the process administration and control.

Change Request Management in SAP Solution Manager is adapted to the processes in the IT Infrastructure Library (ITIL), the de facto standard for Service Management. The aim of Change Request Management is to implement changes economically, in real time, and at minimal risk.

Using Change Request Management in SAP Solution Manager you can enter, categorize, approve, implement, test, and document change requests. In the implementation phase, the integration with the SAP transport system in ABAP and Java reduces the workload of basic tasks for the user. Furthermore, you can save time and costs by bundling the individual change requirements and their implementation in release cycles. The comprehensive reporting functions ensure more transparency and quality in your SAP system landscape.

2.2.6 SAP Service Delivery

To ensure a stable and high-performing system landscape and minimize the risk when running operations, SAP provides various services. SAP services are provided by SAP but can also be implemented for customers by certified SAP partners — both use SAP Solution Manager to perform the service. It is the platform for service delivery.

Now let's distinguish between remote services, onsite services, and self services.

Remote Services

Remote services are, for example, the SAP EarlyWatch Check, SAP GoingLive Check, or SAP OS/DB Migration Check. These are system services within the SAP system landscape in which an experienced SAP consultant dials into your system from a remote location and examines the system according to the requirements of the services you have purchased.

If you use SAP Solution Manager, the services are performed here. This means that in addition to viewing the final report on the services performed, SAP Solution Manager also enables you to view the corresponding individual tasks that were carried out during the service. This ensures a better insight into the service provided. If you need the final report again in the future you can download it from SAP Solution Manager at any time.

Onsite Services

Onsite services are performed at your site by an SAP consultant. Here, the analysis includes a specific part of the system landscape or business processes.

As is the case with remote services, the SAP consultant stores the results and suggested solutions in SAP Solution Manager. For each service provided you can generate a report, which is available in SAP Solution Manager at any time.

Self Services

Self services are not provided by an SAP consultant but by an employee of the customer or partner. As a prerequisite, the employee has to be trained by SAP. In this case the customer himself is responsible for the accuracy of the analysis and the subsequent conclusions. Self services can only be performed in SAP Solution Manager.

SAP Solution Manager enables you to order and be provided with these services. For this reason, it provides the platform via the *Service Delivery* work center (see Figure 2.10). When you select a service, the system displays a description of the service. You can trigger the ordering process directly from the work center.

Issue Management

If a problem (also referred to as an *issue*) has been detected with a service delivery, these problems are mapped and tracked via Issue Management in SAP Solution Manager. However, issues can also occur while running operations. You must differentiate between issues and top issues.

- **Issues**
  An issue is a problem that interrupts operational processing in the short or long term. This issue is reported and processed via a Service Desk message.

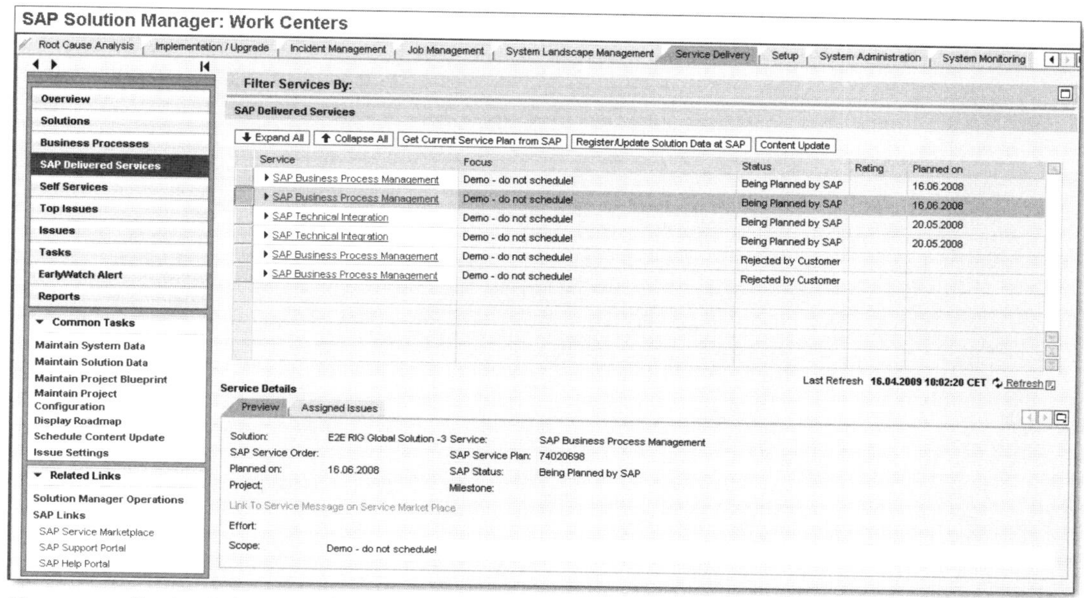

Figure 2.10 Service Delivery Work Center

- **Top issues**
  A top issue is a serious problem. A top issue can also be a set of related problems combined into a complex problem. Top issues always involve a decision at management level.

Issue tracking is an interface between the support organization of the customer and SAP Support. Issue management improves the coordination of the cooperation between the customer support organization and SAP Support.

Service Channel

The SAP Service Channel links SAP Solution Manager and the SAP Service Marketplace. SAP Solution Manager enables you to easily contact SAP directly via this Service Channel.

2.3 ITIL

Future releases of SAP Solution Manager will see a further alignment of terminology and functionalities with the ITIL standards. ITIL is the de facto standard for processes in IT service management. In the service management processes of the current release of SAP Solution Manager these standards are already partly used but they still carry SAP-specific names. Figure 2.11 shows the relationships between SAP functionalities and ITIL processes. In the following sections we will use the commonly used SAP terminology and would like those readers interested in ITIL to use Figure 2.11 as a reference.

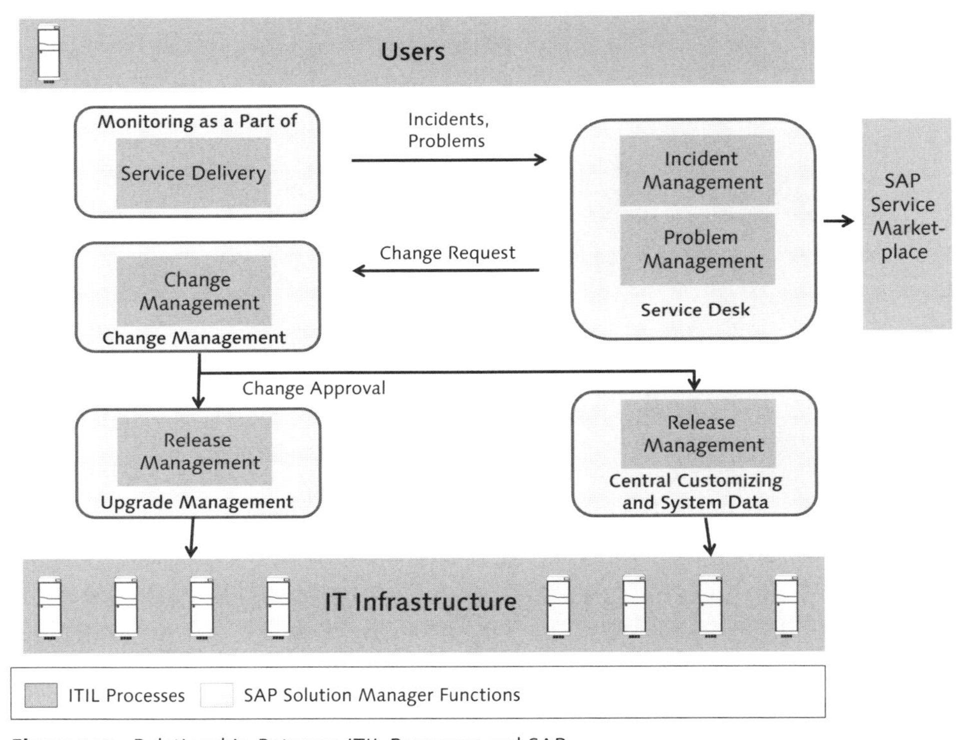

Figure 2.11 Relationship Between ITIL Processes and SAP

2.4 SAP Solution Manager as a Monitoring Tool

Toys Inc. has decided to use SAP Solution Manager 7.0 for its centralized system monitoring. It is the enterprise's top priority to make sure that the system runs at a high performance 24 hours a day according to the system availability requirements.

Why did the management at Toys Inc. decide to use SAP Solution Manager? One important reason is that SAP Solution Manager can be used for both proactive/reactive and manual/automated system monitoring.

- **Proactive system monitoring**
  Before you can do proactive system monitoring you must find out which monitoring objects can become indicators of a possible critical system situation. A critical situation can be avoided if the responsible team takes early action against it. As shown in Figure 2.12, SAP Solution Manager provides you with a corresponding graphic. This graphic displays the overall status of the systems and their components and it enables you to request detailed information about individual monitoring objects.
- **Reactive system monitoring**
  The term reactive means that corrective action is taken only after a critical event has occurred. To do this, you need indicators that signal the occurrence of such events. When used as the central monitoring system SAP Solution Manager provides the functionality to send messages from a central location to the relevant person in charge. This simply means that if a specific system alarm is triggered that is linked to an automatic message; this message is immediately sent from SAP Solution Manager. Such a message can be an email or a Student Management System (SMS).
- **Automated system monitoring**
  Automated system monitoring is done via the Alert Monitor. The Alert Monitor is part of the Computing Center Management System (CCMS). It supports the monitoring and operation of individual components in a system landscape. SAP Solution Manager refers to the monitoring architecture of the CCMS. From here it retrieves information about specific monitoring objects. To perform automated monitoring you must first define monitoring attributes and their threshold values.
- **Manual system monitoring**
  For manual system monitoring you must have profound professional expertise. This is why only administrators and other experts perform this kind of monitoring as they often have experience in various areas of system monitoring and systems analysis. Not only are they able to identify critical system states but can recommend solutions that help avoid such problems.

Manual system monitoring is done in dedicated monitoring screens. For example, in an SAP environment you can use Transaction ST03N to call the Workload Monitor. Here, statistical data about response times, memory usage, database accesses, and so on is collected and stored for each transaction. This data is then summarized and can be used to examine the load distribution within an SAP system.

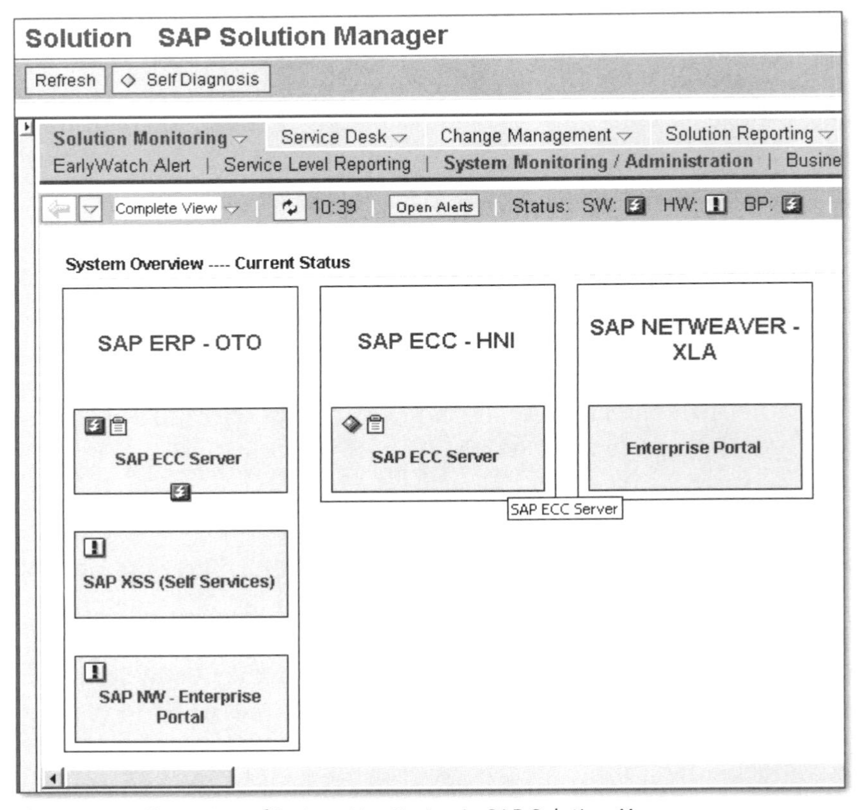

Figure 2.12 Illustration of System Monitoring in SAP Solution Manager

3 Designing the Monitoring Concepts

The monitoring concept forms the basis of system monitoring in a landscape. As described in Chapter 1, The Problem and a Sample Scenario, the implementation of system monitoring requires the scope of a project and should be documented accordingly. In this project, you define the monitoring criteria, alarm processes, and responsibilities.

This chapter provides basic information for designing a monitoring concept and — on the basis of the system landscape at Toys Inc. — lists several necessary monitoring objects as integral parts of this concept. The list contains specific monitoring objects, and you can use it as a basis for your own concept. Please note that this chapter does not provide you with a comprehensive monitoring concept as different kinds of system information can play an important role in monitoring due to the different requirements of system operations and the use of additional SAP and non-SAP components that are not discussed in this book.

This chapter addresses those readers that are interested in general information about a monitoring concept and system administrators responsible for system monitoring.

3.1 The Monitoring Concept

The monitoring concept is the initial system monitoring document. It details the specific system monitoring requirements, the organization of personnel, and the way in which various processes flow within system monitoring work, for example, troubleshooting or escalation procedures.

You constantly have to adapt the document to keep it in line with new developments and changes to the overall process. It should be used as a guide for responsibilities, rules for specific activities, escalation procedures, and the like. Therefore, you should appoint a responsible person to deal with change requests and innovations regarding system monitoring. This person checks the necessity of a change and adapts the monitoring concept, if necessary.

Even though some may not see this as particularly important, you should make sure that the document can be accessed by all of the people involved in system monitoring. Both contact persons and those who are directly involved in system monitoring should be able to access it from a central location. Suppose an escalation process needs to be triggered. The person responsible for this has just joined the enterprise and there's no one to provide information about the escalation process. In such a case, what options would be available to you to react within a given timeframe? The answer is easy: follow the instructions in the concept document.

The following sections describe the components that can be part of a monitoring concept. They are meant to be suggestions and pointers for you if you have to develop a monitoring concept for your own system landscape to serve the requirements of both users and yourself.

3.1.1 Requirements of System Monitoring

The first part of the monitoring concept should describe the general requirements of system monitoring. This part should not contain any further details, such as the specification of monitoring objects and their threshold values; it should instead consider those issues that regularly caused problems in the past and that might affect a smooth system operation in the future. Examples would include a constantly poor response time due to a continuously high load on the memory of different applications or even the standstill of a system due to lack of disk storage. It is advisable that the project group clarify these items from their first meeting. Toward the end of the concept design phase you should make sure the list of requirements has been included in its entirety in the concept.

3.1.2 Documenting the System Landscape

When designing the monitoring concept it is important that you get a complete overview of the system landscape. The overview should contain a presentation of the landscape structure that either includes all systems in use or only those systems that are required for a productive system operation. The systems included in the structural overview differ in each individual landscape. However, it is strongly recommended that you include all your systems in it. Thus, upon completion of the monitoring concept, your documentation will be comprehensive. And please don't forget that this documentation will later serve as the basis for setting up the system landscape in SAP Solution Manager. The more details you consider, the less time needed for additional information gathering during the setup phase. It is completely up to you to select the form of documentation. Toys Inc. selected the SAP standard and uses the *standard minimum documentation* for the monitoring concept. This documentation is also used within the scope of *Run SAP* projects. This type of documentation assumes that the information is not supposed to be recorded redundantly. Only as much information as is needed for the project is supposed to be gathered. However, the information must be detailed in such a way that it can be used by other projects to avoid a new maintenance effort.

For reasons of clarity you should divide the system landscape into several areas according to the application components used, as described in Table 3.1. Here, the SAP application components are considered with regard to our sample enterprise, Toys Inc.

SAP Application Component	Product Release	SID	Installation Number	System Description
SAP ECC 6.0	7.00	OTO	0020096422	Production system
SAP ECC 6.0	7.00	ETO	0020096423	Development system
SAP ECC 6.0	7.00	TTO	0020096424	Test system
SAP NW BW	7.0	PBI	0120003412	Production system
SAP NW BW	7.0	DBI	0120003413	Development system
SAP NW BW	7.0	TBI	0120003414	Test system
SAP SCM	5.0	TEC	0120003412	Production system
SAP SCM	5.0	DEC	0120003413	Development system
SAP SCM	5.0	AEC	0120003414	Test system
SAP NW Portal	7.0	PS1	0020005530	Production system (Web shop)
SAP NW Portal	7.0	TS1	0020005530	Test system

Table 3.1 SAP System Landscape at Toys Inc.

Depending on the solution implemented, an SAP application can contain additional technical components apart from the central database. For example, in SAP Supply Chain Management (SCM) 5.0 you can use Advanced Planning and Optimization (APO), Inventory Collaboration Hub (ICH), Forecast & Replenishment (F&R), Extended Warehouse Management (EWM), or Event Manager (EM).

If you use APO — as we do in our example with Toys Inc. — you need liveCache, a technical component that runs on the same host as the APO solution. You can also use liveCache on a different host, that is, as distinct from your APO solution. As an option, you can also use so-called *optimizers* with your APO solution. But this depends on the type of applications you use within the APO solution. Table 3.2 summarizes these technical components.

SID	Component	Server	Release	Name
TEC	liveCache	us4118	7.4.2.20	TEC
DEC	liveCache	us4119	7.4.2.20	DEC
AEC	liveCache	us4120	7.4.2.20	AEC

Table 3.2 Additional APO Components of the System Landscape at Toys Inc.

A third overview should contain hardware information for the SAP systems. The information should include the server names, the hardware vendor, the server model, the number of CPUs, the size of the main memory, and the operating system, including its version number. Table 3.3 contains an overview of the hardware configuration at Toys Inc. Each SAP system runs on a separate machine.

Another important aspect is the description of the database systems in use, including their version numbers. You should also create an overview for this information. Table 3.4 shows that Toys Inc. uses the SAP MaxDB database system for all of its systems. The databases of the individual systems run on the same machine as the applications used.

SAP and non-SAP systems are part of the overall solution. Thus, the relevant information also has to be collected for the non-SAP systems. Table 3.5 shows the warehouse management solution (WAMA) at Toys Inc., for which the product WAMA is used.

SID of the Solution	Instance	Server Name	Hardware Vendors	Server Model	CPU Frequency (MHz)	RAM (GB)	Operating System, Version
OTO	bsl1041_ OTO_20	bsl1041	ABC Enterprises	Saturn 2x1800	1,800	10	Linux — SLES 9
ETO	bsl1042_ ETO_20	bsl1042	ABC Enterprises	Saturn 2x1800	1,800	10	Linux — SLES 9
TTO	bsl1043_ TTO_20	bsl1043	ABC Enterprises	Saturn 2x1800	1,800	10	Linux — SLES 9
PBI	nb- itc-0301_ PBI_10	nb- itc-0301	ABC Enterprises	Jupiter 900	1,600	12	Linux — SLES 10
DBI	nb- itc-0302_ DBI_10	nb-itc- 0302	ABC Enterprises	Jupiter 900	1,600	12	Linux — SLES 10
TBI	nb- itc-0303_ TBI_10	nb-itc- 0303	ABC Enterprises	Jupiter 900	1,600	12	Linux — SLES 10
TEC	us4118_ TEC_01	us4118	ABC Enterprises	Jupiter 900	1,600	10	Linux — SLES 9
DEC	us4119_ DEC_01	us4119	ABC Enterprises	Jupiter 900	1,600	10	Linux — SLES 9
AEC	us4120_ AEC_01	us4120	ABC Enterprises	Jupiter 900	1,600	10	Linux — SLES 9
PS1	wdfd 00208475a_ PS1_10	wdfd 00208 475a	ABC Enterprises	Mercury 1200	1,600	8	MS Windows NT 5.0
TS1	wdfd00208 475b_TS1_ 10	wdfd 00208 475b	ABC Enterprises	Mercury 1200	1,600	8	MS Windows NT 5.0

Table 3.3 Hardware Overview of the SAP System Landscape at Toys Inc.

SID	Database Server	Database System, Version
OTO	bsl1041	SAP MaxDB 7.6
ETO	bsl1042	SAP MaxDB 7.6
TTO	bsl1043	SAP MaxDB 7.6
PBI	nb-itc-0301	SAP MaxDB 7.6
DBI	nb-itc-0302	SAP MaxDB 7.6
TBI	nb-itc-0303	SAP MaxDB 7.6
TEC	us4118	SAP MaxDB 7.6
DEC	us4119	SAP MaxDB 7.6
AEC	us4120	SAP MaxDB 7.6
PS1	wdfd00208475a	SAP MaxDB 7.6
TS1	wdfd00208475b	SAP MaxDB 7.6

Table 3.4 Database Overview of the SAP System Landscape at Toys Inc.

SID	Product/ Version	Vendor	Server Name	Description
WAMA	WAMA 01	Outside Inc.	PDFA040	Warehouse management system

Table 3.5 Overview of Non-SAP Systems as Part of the Overall Solution at Toys Inc.

Table 3.6 contains an overview of the hardware configuration, on the basis of which the WAMA solution has been implemented.

SID of the Solution	WAMA
Server Name	WAMA99
Hardware Vendors	ABC Enterprises
Server Model	Mars 1200
CPU Frequency (MHz)	1.200
Memory (GB)	16
Operating System, Version	MS Windows NT 5.0

Table 3.6 Hardware Overview of Non-SAP Systems in the Overall Solution at Toys Inc.

3.1.3 Defining Roles and Responsibilities

If centralized system monitoring exists, you must appoint a person with sole responsibility for them. If possible, this person should also constantly maintain the monitoring concept and act as the point of contact regarding system monitoring.

In addition, you should create documentation with the names of the contact persons for the system monitoring group. A possible breakdown of the persons responsible can look as shown in Table 3.7. Due to today's highly developed, heterogeneous system landscapes, the assignment of responsibilities for system landscapes may be different in every enterprise. Based on historical developments, Toys Inc. opted for the following structure for the monitoring concept. As you can see, there's only one contact person for each area within the team.

Team	Contact for	Name of Contact	Phone/ Mail
Basis team	Database management system	...	...
	Operating system management	...	...
	Backup/recovery	...	...
	Hardware management	...	...
	Network management	...	...
	Security management	...	...
Help desk team	Front-end support	...	...
Warehouse management team	Application management	...	...
	Performance monitoring	...	...
	Interface management	...	...
	Background processing	...	...
SAP team	ERP Central Component (ECC) basis	...	...
	Business Warehouse (BW) basis		
	Basis Enterprise Portal (EP)		
	Basis SCM		
	Interface management	...	...
	Background processing	...	...
	Application management	...	...

Table 3.7 Directory of Contact Persons for System Monitoring Responsibilities at Toys Inc.

If your enterprise cooperates with outsourcing service providers, you must also assign the monitoring tasks. Customers usually use the Service Desk as a point of contact. If the Service Desk is at the outsourcer or if the outsourcer is responsible for the functioning of certain services within a system, the list of the responsible contact persons should be compiled accordingly.

A system consultant cannot work on a 24/7 basis. Therefore, you should organize a stand-by service that can be called instead of the system consultant in case of emergency.

3.1.4 Defining Monitoring Processes

To define the monitoring processes, you must first describe the process. The following should be noted:

- **Basic conditions for the monitoring process**
  For example, you have to define the number of hours needed per day for the complete monitoring process. This depends, to a certain degree, on how long the systems have to be available each day and at what times; moreover, it is important to know what effects to expect if the monitoring of specific system components is continued the following day. In general, it can be said that in most companies there is a stand-by service that can be notified via text messages or pager in the case of serious problems, even in those companies that haven't implemented any continuous system monitoring.
- **Executing the monitoring process**
  There must be clarification on how the system monitoring process is executed. In this respect you must specify what needs to be monitored and at what intervals. The person that carries out the system monitoring needs instructions on how to respond to alarms or how and to whom he can transfer an incident.
- **Troubleshooting/escalation process**
  What happens when an alarm has been triggered? You have to react. An immediate incident analysis might be initiated or the incident may be solved after the alarm was triggered. In the worst case, you must start an escalation procedure because the problem is so severe it brings the business-critical processes to a standstill because it cannot be solved within the given timeframe. In this case, you need both an alarm and a business continuity plan. You have to define which people are to be involved in the escalation process and what actions

need to be taken during the escalation. Also, in a serious case you must plan in advance how you can keep the business running in this situation, for example, with manual means.

3.1.5 Monitoring Objects

In technical monitoring, monitoring objects are components within an information technology (IT) environment, such as the memory of a server or the background processing. Every monitoring object possesses specific attributes. For example, these attributes can be measurement values, statuses or messages, the memory utilization, or the average runtime of a background job.

There are many different monitoring objects within a system monitoring process. But the trick is to identify those that are really necessary to ensure a smooth system operation of an application. As described in Section 3.1.1, Requirements of System Monitoring, the catalog of requirements serves as the basis for the selection of monitoring objects; and any existing agreements (service level agreements (SLAs)) regarding system availability and system performance that might have been made between the IT department and the specialist department, play an equally important role.

To facilitate a targeted selection of monitoring objects, you should create an overview of the required characteristics in advance. System monitoring involves various factors; for the initial selection, however, the objects should not play a role yet. To obtain an overview, you should first structure the areas and their importance within system monitoring as shown in Table 3.8.

Category	Area	Priority
Operating systems	File systems	High
	CPU	High
	Memory	High
SAP NetWeaver AS ABAP	Instance availability	Management
Background processing	Jobs	High
ABAP dumps	ABAP	Medium

Table 3.8 Categorizing and Prioritizing the Monitoring Objects

The target selection of objects and their prioritization is carried out in the main part of the monitoring concept. Section 3.2, Operating System, includes the areas listed in Table 3.8 and uses them as the basis for structuring the monitoring concept.

Toys Inc. selected its monitoring objects with regard to the risk of the business processes to counteract the already-allocated problems in time. The selection made can be used as a basis for many scenarios, but should be supplemented by some objects.

3.1.6 Threshold-Value Definitions

An important prerequisite for automated system monitoring is appropriate threshold-value definitions. They help you define the exact point at which an alarm for a monitoring attribute is generated when the value exceeds or falls below the threshold. Threshold-value definitions are specified in different units, for example, in percent, milliseconds, or as a quantity.

As a kind of preparation for defining and integrating the threshold values in the SAP Solution Manager system, Table 3.9 shows the four different threshold values for a monitoring attribute that exist in the monitoring console of an SAP environment.

Threshold Value	Presentation in the Monitoring Console
Green to yellow	Yellow
Yellow to red	Red
Red to yellow	Yellow
Yellow to green	Green

Table 3.9 Threshold Values in the SAP Monitoring Console

An attribute that currently possesses the alert color green changes its alert color to yellow when it exceeds or falls below the threshold value. It changes to red when it exceeds or falls below the threshold value for the red alarm status. This color change also occurs the other way around in case of an all-clear.

If the value of an attribute constantly fluctuates above or below a certain threshold value, the alert status may constantly change. To avoid this you can assign different threshold values for a change from green to yellow and from yellow to green. The same applies to the change from yellow to red and vice versa.

Once you have defined the monitoring objects to include in the system monitoring process you define the corresponding threshold values as shown in Table 3.10.

For example, if the file system is used at more than 90%, then the alert color will change from green to yellow. If the utilization increases to 98% or higher, then the alert color will change from yellow to red. If action is taken in response to the alarm and free space is created, then the alert color will change from red back to yellow when the value falls below 95%. Once the threshold value of 85% has been reached the alert color will again change from yellow to green. Table 3.10 provides three further examples for threshold values: For the Free storage space in the file system attribute, an alarm is triggered when the values fall below the threshold, for the CPU utilization and Number of jobs canceled when the thresholds are exceeded.

	Threshold Values			
Monitoring Attribute	**Green to yellow**	**Yellow to red**	**Red to yellow**	**Yellow to green**
Free storage space in the file system	7%	5%	7%	10%
CPU utilization	60%	80%	75%	55%
Number of jobs canceled	5	10	9	2

Table 3.10 Overview of a Sample Threshold-Value Definition

3.1.7 Monitoring Frequency

The next thing you have to clarify is how often the attribute of the monitoring object has to be monitored. You must first differentiate between automated and manual system monitoring. Automated system monitoring is checked continuously. Objects that are monitored manually can be checked on a daily, weekly, monthly, yearly basis, or as needed.

The instance availability, for example, has to be ensured continuously and should therefore be included in constant system monitoring. It is a good idea to create an overview of your monitoring attributes and the corresponding periods in which they have to be checked (see Table 3.11).

Monitoring Attribute	Monitoring Frequency
Instance availability	Continuous
Free space requirement of file system	Continuous
Average response time of dialog service	Weekly
Database growth	Monthly

Table 3.11 Overview of the Monitoring Frequencies for Monitoring Attributes

3.1.8 Alert Notification

In the event of an alarm, monitoring objects that have a high priority should also be equipped with a notification method.

If an alarm is triggered and becomes visible in SAP Solution Manager, an auto-response method is supposed to be started, which is sent to either a predefined number of people or only to the person in charge of system monitoring who, in turn, initiates all further alarm procedures according to specified instructions.

3.2 Operating System (OS)

At the OS level there are some important components that you have to include in the system monitoring process, because the occurrence of problems may result in a chain reaction and affect the entire system landscape, which can eventually lead to a complete system standstill.

The final part of each of the following sections contains an overview table that summarizes the most important characteristics of the corresponding component with regard to system monitoring.

3.2.1 File System

The file system consists of various files that are structured according to their purpose. Any problem that occurs in the file system has an effect upon the entire process flow of an application. It is therefore essential that you include the file system in your centralized system monitoring process. The main reason to do so is to monitor the available free hard disk space in the file system or — vice versa — the percentage of used space (see Table 3.12). A file system without any free space can lead to an application standstill as no additional information can be stored or modified within the file system.

Category	Operating system
Monitoring object	File system
Monitoring attribute of the object	Free space requirement of file system
Responsibility	Centralized system monitoring
Type of monitoring	Automated
Autoreaction method	Yes

Table 3.12 Monitoring the Use of Disk Space in the File System

3.2.2 CPU

Systems with a constantly high utilization of CPU resources can have a negative impact on the response times and the performance of a system landscape, which is why it is important to monitor the average use of a system's CPUs.

If you detect a high CPU utilization it doesn't necessarily mean that there is a hardware bottleneck, as the causes for this high utilization value can be manifold. You need to distinguish between a continuously high utilization of CPU resources and a temporary one. This means that when you receive an alarm for high CPU utilization you must discover the underlying problem. As a rule of thumb, you can say that over the period of one hour the free portion of CPU should have an average value of at least 20%. A value of 35% of free CPU capacity would be even more desirable. For an analysis, SAP provides different monitors, such as the OS monitor (Transaction ST06) and the workload monitor (Transaction ST03N) (see Table 3.13).

Category	Operating system
Monitoring object	CPU
Monitoring attribute of the object	Average CPU utilization
Responsibility	Centralized system monitoring
Type of monitoring	Automated
Autoreaction method	No

Table 3.13 Monitoring the Average CPU Utilization

3.2.3 Main Memory and Paging Behavior

Monitoring the utilization of the main memory is just as important as monitoring the CPU utilization. Bottlenecks of the main memory can be made visible by moving the memory pages to a hard disk (paging). Here, we have another rule of thumb: If less than 20% of physical memory is stored in a paging file on a hard disk, you can consider the situation as not critical.

High paging rates occur when too many processes are run on the system or when there's not enough memory available for running processes. Similar to what was described for the CPU utilization you must check if the paging of processes has a negative effect on the system response times and whether the system's performance is deteriorating. Based on the results, you must decide whether a more comprehensive analysis is necessary.

Please note that different OSs have different characteristics. It is not always the case that a high paging rate means that there is a memory bottleneck. It is also important to know if a high paging rate can be found on several different machines or only on a specific one and also, whether you are dealing with a general problem or a specific one that extensively allocates memory.

In their classic definition, paging and swapping were two terms from different OS worlds: Windows and Unix. Today, this differentiation has become obsolete due to modern memory management technologies. Originally, swapping refers to the complete moving of a process to an extended memory of a Unix system; paging, by contrast, means the partial moving of individual memory pages to an extended memory (separate hard disk area). Because the principle of moving partial processes and individual memory pages has proven itself in Windows systems, it was also integrated with Unix systems in modern processors. Therefore, the boundaries between the terms paging and swapping are now blurred (see Tables 3.14 and 3.15).

Category	Operating system
Monitoring object	Memory utilization — paging
Monitoring attribute of the object	Average memory utilization
Responsibility	Centralized system monitoring
Type of monitoring	Automated
Autoreaction method	No

Table 3.14 Monitoring the Average Memory Utilization

Category	Operating system (Linux/Unix)
Monitoring object	Swap space
Monitoring attribute of the object	Utilization of the allocated storage space on the hard disk
Responsibility	Centralized system monitoring
Type of monitoring	Automated
Autoreaction method	No

Table 3.15 Monitoring the Use of Swap Space

3.2.4 OS Collector

The OS collector runs on every SAP application server and database system. The SAPOSCOL program collects OS system data that is then transmitted to the monitoring architecture. It is advisable to monitor the status of the OS collector because otherwise no operating system data is collected (see Table 3.16).

Category	OS
Monitoring object	OS collector
Monitoring attribute of the object	Status of the OS collector
Responsibility	Centralized system monitoring
Type of monitoring	Automated
Autoreaction method	Yes

Table 3.16 Monitoring the OS Collector Status

3.3 System and Instance Availability

Basically, every enterprise wants to keep the costs for its data centers as low as possible. But the expectations of users and the demands on the systems are high. The systems have to be available around the clock, which is not always possible due to limited budgets. Especially if a 24/7 availability has to be ensured, it is reasonable to consider the implementation of sophisticated high-availability solutions, such as server mirroring or a clustering solution. The related costs, though, are very high.

Regardless of the question whether a system has to be available for 12 or 24 hours, you should include the monitoring of the systems' availability and their application servers into the centralized monitoring process. By doing this you make sure that the systems are available in the required timeframe and work without any problems.

Let's recall the problems that occurred previously in the system monitoring process at Toys Inc. and were recorded by their project group (see Chapter 1, Section 1.4, Toys Inc.: Initial Situation). A very important aspect was the response time regarding the problem identification in the case of a system availability failure in a 24/7 system operation. A system failure should not first be noted by users or other persons who don't deal with the system operation. The system administrator should be the first to notice the problem.

In the SAP environment you can use the availability agent CCMSPING to check the availability of the message server. If the system is active, the message server will respond to the request of the availability agent. At the same time, this means that at least one application server has been registered as active in the message server (see Table 3.17).

Category	System and instance availability
Monitoring object I	System availability
Monitoring object II	Instance availability
Monitoring attribute of the object I	Availability per system
Monitoring attribute of the object II	Status of instance availability
Responsibility	Centralized system monitoring
Type of monitoring	Automated
Auto-reaction method	Yes

Table 3.17 Monitoring the System and Instance Availability

Availability of Online Applications

Toys Inc. uses SAP NetWeaver Portal to operate a Web shop and a portal for suppliers. Therefore, it is important to Toys Inc. to monitor these two accesses with regard to their availability. If one of the applications would fail for system reasons, this would cause enormous financial loss of sales. To monitor the Internet presence, Toys Inc. uses the *Generic Request and Message Generator* (GRMG) agent for querying the URLs to receive performance information about the call (see Table 3.18).

Category	System and instance availability
Monitoring object I	Process availability
Monitoring attribute of the object I	Availability per process
Monitoring attribute of the object II	Status of the Web process availability
Responsibility	Centralized system monitoring
Type of monitoring	Automated
Autoreaction method	Yes

Table 3.18 Monitoring the Availability of Web Presences

3.4 Background Processing

Although there is increasing tendency toward dialog-oriented processes, a large number of them still run in the background. The IT systems are available 24/7 for dialog and online processes, but background processes must be scheduled for times with low loads. This requires not only precise planning but also monitoring that is continuously active in the dialog applications and background application areas.

There are two different areas when monitoring background processes:

The first one is a rather global view of background processing. It mainly focuses on:

- the average utilization of the background work processes of a server
- the number of errors in background work processes
- the program errors during the execution of background jobs
- the number of jobs canceled on an application server

The second area focuses on monitoring specific jobs. You check if the scheduled jobs were run correctly, the runtime behavior, you check if jobs have to be rescheduled or activated manually, if they have to be run again, and which jobs were canceled. For jobs that can have a substantial effect on a system's performance it would be good to install the automatic notification function. Table 3.19 illustrates the system-wide monitoring of the background process, Table 3.20 lists the background processing per application server as an example, and Table 3.21 includes the attributes for dedicated jobs.

Category	Background processing
Monitoring object	Background processing service — system-wide
Monitoring attribute of the object	Number of jobs ready to run and authorized to start
Responsibility	Centralized system monitoring
Type of monitoring	Automated
Autoreaction method	No

Table 3.19 Monitoring the System-Wide Background Processing

Category	Background processing
Monitoring object	Background processing service — per application server
Monitoring attribute I of the object	Average utilization of background processes
Monitoring attribute II of the object	Number of errors in background work processes
Monitoring attribute III of the object	Program errors during the execution of background jobs
Monitoring attribute IV of the object	Number of jobs canceled on an application server
Responsibility	Centralized system monitoring
Type of monitoring	Automated
Autoreaction method	No

Table 3.20 Monitoring the Background Processing per Application Server

In addition to the general criteria for monitoring background processes described earlier, the use and integration of a job scheduler into your system monitoring model should also be considered. A job scheduler, also called a background-processing control system, automatically starts and monitors background processes.

Category	Background processing
Monitoring object	Background processing — per job
Monitoring attribute I of the object	Runtime of the job
Monitoring attribute II of the object	Time delay until job starts
Monitoring attribute III of the object	Job status
Responsibility	Centralized system monitoring
Type of monitoring	Automated
Autoreaction method	Yes (depending on the importance of the job)

Table 3.21 Monitoring the Background Processing per Job

When you use a job scheduler you not only define the specific jobs themselves but also the processes that enable you to restart jobs after a failure or to respond appropriately if individual batch runs build on each other and consequently reschedule follow-up jobs. Even in the case of a complete system failure, job schedulers are able to reorganize the job chains due to processes you had previously defined.

However, despite all of this automation, the system administrators still need to monitor the background processing. For example, they have to manually restart background jobs that repeatedly started automatically and were not fully completed.

3.5 System Performance

If you continuously monitor the performance of your system, you can identify and avoid problems before they occur. There are many reasons for problems with system performance. Perhaps your hardware is not configured to handle the existing loads or the configuration of your entire system is not optimal. Possibly, only some specific programs that you use are very time intensive and use a lot of system resources so that a few changed settings could help improve the overall performance. Or a database performance problem could be the cause. To find the right solutions for SAP systems you first have to do a workload analysis. To support the workload analysis, the SAP landscapes provide the End-to-End Root Cause Analysis tools. They use existing information from the workload monitor (Transaction ST03N) of the SAP AS ABAP systems and Wily Introscope performance information for SAP systems with a Java instance. This information is provided to the analysis tools centrally. It provides you with information about response time behaviors, throughput, and loads in an SAP system. You should use this tool as the first step of an extensive and detailed analysis.

Possible performance problems may occur in dialog operation, background processing (see Section 3.4), spool service, and update service. Tables 3.22, 3.23, 3.24, 3.25, and 3.26 include select information from possible monitoring objects that are monitored for each application server. These monitoring objects refer to the general system performance. Using this information you make initial conclusions and perform additional detailed analyses in the case of an alarm.

If you need further detailed information about SAP performance optimization, you should refer to the latest edition of *SAP Performance Optimization* by Thomas Schneider, also published by SAP PRESS. No matter which SAP solution you have to manage, Thomas Schneider's book helps you to systematically identify and analyze performance problems for any SAP solution and to come up with a solution approach.

For many users an important value is still the average response time of a transactional step in a dialog. Therefore, it can be found both in the service contracts with hosting enterprises and internally between the IT department and the application owners. Based on this criterion, you frequently evaluate the system performance of a system over a given period of time. For example, in an ERP system the performance is good if the average dialog response time is approximately one second. However, due to different requirements of the systems set by different business processes and also due to the individual configuration of a system landscape, it is impossible to use this rule for all enterprise systems or every SAP solution (SAP SCM, SAP Customer Relationship Management (CRM), SAP NetWeaver BW, SAP EP, and so on). On the contrary, every system landscape must be regarded individually. Depending on the SAP solution you have implemented, the average dialog response time can vary considerably. As a kind of reference value you can use the ratio between the average response time and the average database time in dialog operation mode. If the value for the database time is more than 40% higher than that for the average response time, this could be an indication of a possible database or network problem, or a CPU bottleneck.

Toys Inc. decided to add the most important transactions to their monitoring. This way, it is possible to report the performance information periodically to better identify and assess the developments within the system.

Category	System performance (ABAP)
Monitoring object	Dialog service
Monitoring attribute II of the object	Average use of dialog work processes of an application server
Monitoring attribute II of the object	Average database time of dialog service
Monitoring attribute IV of the object	Number of dialog work processes in PRIV mode
Monitoring attribute V of the object	Wait time in the dispatcher queue
Monitoring attribute VI of the object	Time for long-lasting dialog work processes
Responsibility	Centralized system monitoring
Type of monitoring	Automated
Autoreaction method	No

Table 3.22 Monitoring the Dialog Service

Category	System performance (ABAP)
Monitoring object	Updating — system-wide
Monitoring attribute of the object	Number of wrong update requests
Responsibility	Centralized system monitoring
Type of monitoring	Automated
Autoreaction method	Yes

Table 3.23 Monitoring Updating — System-Wide

Category	System performance (ABAP)
Monitoring object	Updating — per application server
Monitoring attribute I of the object	Wait time in the dispatcher queue
Monitoring attribute II of the object	Utilization of update work processes
Monitoring attribute III of the object	Update error in work process
Responsibility	Centralized system monitoring
Type of monitoring	Automated
Autoreaction method	No

Table 3.24 Monitoring Updating per Application Server

Category	System performance (Java)
Monitoring object	Average response time
Monitoring attribute I of the object	Response time of servlets
Monitoring attribute II of the object	Response time of Web Dynpros
Monitoring attribute III of the object	JCo calls (database calls)
Responsibility	Centralized system monitoring
Type of monitoring	Manual
Autoreaction method	No

Table 3.25 Monitoring the Response Times per Java Instance

Category	System performance (Java)
Monitoring object	Java Virtual Machine — memory usage
Monitoring attribute I of the object	Used memory
Monitoring attribute II of the object	Garbage collection runtime
Responsibility	Centralized system monitoring
Type of monitoring	Manual
Autoreaction method	No

Table 3.26 Monitoring the Memory Utilization per Java Instance

3.6 Spool Service

The spool service controls all output processes of an AS ABAP system, including print control. At Toys Inc., the creation of requests for payment was incorporated along with all of the critical processes of the enterprise. Due to the very large customer base of Toys Inc., the enterprise requires an output process with low wait time. For Toys Inc., the printout is a business-critical process that must be monitored with appropriate care. Table 3.27 shows the typical monitoring objects that were selected for monitoring.

Category	System performance
Monitoring object	Spool service
Monitoring attribute I of the object	Wait time of spool work processes

Table 3.27 Monitoring the Spool Service

Monitoring attribute II of the object	Used spool numbers of SPO_NUM number range in the system
Responsibility	Centralized system monitoring
Type of monitoring	Automated
Autoreaction method	No

Table 3.27 Monitoring the Spool Service (Cont.)

3.7 Traces

Traces are used to monitor the system and to isolate problems that occur in an SAP system. Traces can be activated for both ABAP and Java. Different tools are required for each. When you switch on a trace in an AS ABAP system, various operations of an application are logged depending on the corresponding level. There are two types of traces — *developer traces* and *performance traces* — that are activated directly in the system. For AS Java systems, traces are created using the End-to-End Root Cause Analysis tools and displayed in Solution Manager Diagnostics.

However, you should only use the trace functions in exceptional circumstances because they could affect system performance due to the increased write activities. Therefore, you should check on a daily basis if the traces are switched on and if so, whether they have an effect on the system operation and could be deactivated.

Table 3.28 shows the status of the developer traces and performance traces.

Category	Basis
Monitoring object	Trace
Monitoring attribute I of the object	Status of developer trace
Monitoring attribute II of the object	Status of system trace
Responsibility	Centralized system monitoring
Type of monitoring	Automated
Autoreaction method	No

Table 3.28 Monitoring the Trace Functionality

3.8 Memory Management

Using Memory Management you can assign different SAP memory areas within an SAP instance to the applications. The appropriate parameterization enables you to define which memory area is used. During operation hours of an SAP system you should check to see if the necessary resources are available to Memory Management and if the system is slowed down by paging processes or other bottlenecks due to a lack of resources.

The configuration of SAP memory areas plays an important role. If the SAP memory areas are not optimally aligned with the system load requirements, performance will go down and the end user will no longer be able to work efficiently. It should therefore be your objective to optimize the memory configuration and to avoid program failures caused by memory bottlenecks. Consequently, you must include the different memory areas in your system monitoring model.

3.8.1 Buffers

Applications use buffers in the main memory to temporarily store data. It is necessary to have information about the quality and efficiency of critical buffers to maintain and improve a system's performance.

Category	Memory management
Monitoring object	SAP table buffer
Monitoring attribute I of the object	Hit ratio
Monitoring attribute II of the object	Swap rate (swaps)
Monitoring attribute III of the object	Free buffer space
Monitoring attribute IV of the object	Space usage for directories
Responsibility	Centralized system monitoring
Type of monitoring	Automated
Autoreaction method	No

Table 3.29 Monitoring the SAP Buffers

For example, the performance of a system can deteriorate if a table buffer is too small, which can lead to displacements (paging) and unnecessary reloads of the database. A displacement is when an object that is to be loaded into the buffer cannot be entirely loaded because the buffer is too small. In such a case other objects have to be displaced or pushed out of the buffer. As a matter of fact, displacements should never occur in a production system.

An attribute for monitoring SAP buffers is the hit ratio. In a production system you should see a hit ratio of 98% or higher. There are exceptions, however, the single-record and the import/export buffers, which can both be below 98%.

3.8.2 AS ABAP: Paging Memory, Roll Memory, Extended Memory, Heap Memory

Like the SAP buffers, the paging memory, roll memory, extended memory, and the heap memory of AS ABAP are separate SAP memory areas. These memory areas are configured for each SAP instance, and system performance plays an important role.

It is highly recommended that you check all of the following attributes for the SAP memory areas on a weekly basis except for the current number of work processes in private mode and the number of restarts of the dialog work processes since startup due to `abap/heaplimit` being exceeded. If you detect a regular occurrence of this state you must check the memory configuration or find out if application errors are the cause (see Table 3.30).

Category	Memory management
Monitoring object	Memory management
Monitoring attribute I of the object	SAP AS ABAP paging: Maximum utilization of paging area since system startup
Monitoring attribute II of the object	SAP AS ABAP roll: Maximum utilization of roll area since system startup
Monitoring attribute III of the object	High watermark of extended memory since startup
Monitoring attribute IV of the object	Amount of extended memory in user contexts that are currently active in WPs

Table 3.30 Monitoring Additional SAP Memory Areas

Monitoring attribute V of the object	High watermark of heap memory since startup
Monitoring attribute VI of the object	Current number of work processes in PRIV mode
Monitoring attribute VII of the object	Number of dialog-work-process restarts since startup due to excessive `abap/heaplimit`
Responsibility	Centralized system monitoring
Type of monitoring	Automated
Autoreaction method	Yes, for attribute V

Table 3.30 Monitoring Additional SAP Memory Areas (Cont.)

3.9 System Log

All of the activities of an application server are documented in a system log. The system log messages are already subdivided by identification areas (server, system, database); in addition, each message has a unique three-digit identification. This enables you to display specific objects for monitoring. Objects that are not of direct interest can be omitted from alarms and the monitoring system. It is recommended to include messages into the system log monitoring process that affected the operation of your system operation in the past (see Table 3.31).

Category	System logs
Monitoring object	SAP basis system
Monitoring attribute I of the object	Database
Monitoring attribute II of the object	Background processing
Monitoring attribute III of the object	Spool
Monitoring attribute IV of the object	Application
Monitoring attribute V of the object	Communication
Responsibility	Centralized system monitoring
Type of monitoring	Automated
Autoreaction method	Depending on the system message

Table 3.31 Monitoring the System Logs

3.10 Runtime Error

If a runtime error (dump or exception) occurs during the execution of a program, the system generates a log entry. This log entry contains detailed information about the problem and it enables you to perform a detailed analysis. For AS ABAP systems, the information is logged in *dump files* and provided for analysis. AS Java systems use exceptions that originate from Java to display runtime errors in the environment. They are updated in the log files of the system and can be displayed for evaluation using Solution Manager Diagnostics.

It is not unusual for ABAP runtime errors to occur in a development or testing environment. However, in a production system ABAP dumps and Java exceptions should be avoided. If a large number of runtime errors of the same type occur or if a specific type of runtime error that can affect system operations is generated in the production system, you have to perform a more detailed analysis.

There are different types of runtime errors that have different effects on system operations:

- **Memory problems**
  It is possible that runtime errors occur that are related to the memory configuration. This can either be due to an application error or the overall memory configuration is not ideally adapted to the application's requirements. Particularly in AS Java systems, memory problems can occur because of a poor adaptation of the garbage collector.
- **Syntax errors**
  Programs that are modified or newly developed should be tested in the testing system for syntax errors and compatibility problems during both the development phase and upon completion. For example, whether the definition of a variable is missing, if a comma or parenthesis was forgotten in the program, or if an error indicates that the program is unable to run, etc., can all be checked during these tests. If the testing is not properly done in the testing system, problems can occur later in the production system. This means that programs containing syntax errors that haven't been eliminated will certainly fail during operation and have to be reengineered, which will eventually restrict your ability to use the application.
- **Transport errors**
  Let's look at an example:

During the execution of a program a function module cannot be found. The ABAP runtime error reads as follows:

```
CALL_FUNCTION_NOT_FOUND
The "XYZ" function module does not exist.
```

In this example, the `XYZ` function module was called. However, it can't be found in the function library, which there can be several reasons for. One of the reasons could be a transport error. This means it must be checked to see if transports were unsuccessfully imported into the system recently. If that is the case you have to check to see if there are general problems with the transport concept.

- **Authorization problems**
  If a user successfully logs on to a system, it doesn't necessarily mean that he can access all of its different functions. An authorization concept describes the access rights of every user within the system. For example, the concept could specify authorizations with regard to the execution of reports, or the access to specific files and tables, etc.

  The authorization concept prevents users from carrying out activities in the system that could cause problems or even disrupt the entire flow of business activities within an enterprise.

  For example, if a dialog user tries to run a report that calls additional reports and function modules which, in turn, run in the same dialog and involve Remote Function Calls (RFC), this can evoke the RFC_NO_AUTHORITY runtime error provided the user has only limited or perhaps no authorization for RFC calls.

  Table 3.32 lists the monitoring objects for recording the ABAP dump frequency. It is recommended to use the End-to-End Exception Analysis for the analysis of Java runtime errors (see Table 3.33).

Category	ABAP runtime error
Monitoring object	ABAP shortdumps
Monitoring attribute of the object	Number of shortdumps
Responsibility	Centralized system monitoring
Type of monitoring	Automated
Autoreaction method	No

Table 3.32 Monitoring ABAP Dumps

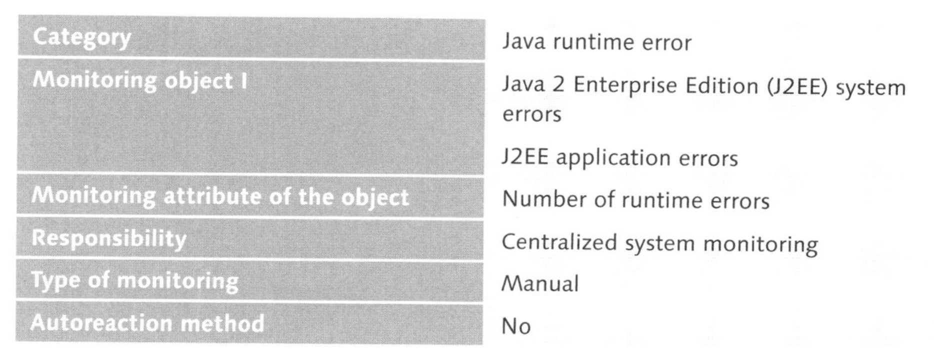

Category	Java runtime error
Monitoring object I	Java 2 Enterprise Edition (J2EE) system errors J2EE application errors
Monitoring attribute of the object	Number of runtime errors
Responsibility	Centralized system monitoring
Type of monitoring	Manual
Autoreaction method	No

Table 3.33 Monitoring Runtime Errors in AS Java

3.11 User Monitoring — System Security

Every enterprise wants to stay in control of its systems. This involves preventing unnoticed access to the system by strangers. Needless to say that there is no absolute secure system landscape with regard to attacks from the outside. Computers and applications, such as OSs, are made by humans and it quite often happens that security concepts are quickly discarded due to idleness or inattentiveness.

We distinguish between two areas of security: the security of the machines themselves, and possible attacks from the network or the Internet. Both of these areas require you to take precautionary measures.

For example, an authorization concept ensures the security of the systems. According to their roles, system users should be granted the relevant authorizations. And only those. Another aspect is the creation of secure passwords. Usually, administrators are much more aware of this security problem than the "normal" users who often tend to use passwords that stem from their social environment and don't contain any cryptic letter combinations.

Do you have an idea of how secure the programs are that you use? Actually, you can never be sure that your software doesn't bear any risks. Outside attackers will always try to utilize program weaknesses. In the final analysis this means that you should also check the passwords of all users regularly to see if they are good enough.

The SAP software provides only a few rudimentary security checks, which should be used. You should regularly check how many users have tried to log on to a particular system — and not only for purely statistical reasons. It is much more important to identify the number of failed logons and the number of locks due to incorrect logon details. A large number of failed logons might indicate that someone is systematically trying to enter your system from the outside. In addition, it must be ensured that users who repeatedly fail to log on successfully are locked at the right time. Table 3.34 suggests some possible monitoring attributes that can be included into the default system monitoring process.

Category	User monitoring
Monitoring object	Logons
Monitoring attribute I of the object	Successful logon of a user
Monitoring attribute II of the object	Failed logon of a user
Monitoring attribute III of the object	Locking of a user due to failed logon
Monitoring attribute IV of the object	RFC/CPIC logon successful
Monitoring attribute V of the object	RFC/CPIC logon failed
Responsibility	Centralized system monitoring
Type of monitoring	Automated
Autoreaction method	No

Table 3.34 Monitoring SAP System Logons

A second aspect of system security is the security of the network. A number of tools help you to monitor and inspect the network traffic. For example, these are tools that "eavesdrop" on the data traffic. Others check specific services, such as open ports of machines or within networks (see Table 3.35).

Category	Network monitoring
Monitoring object	Network communication
Monitoring attribute I of the object	Open ports
Monitoring attribute II of the object	Collisions on the network
Responsibility	Local system monitoring
Type of monitoring	Manual
Autoreaction method	No

Table 3.35 Monitoring the Network Communication in the System Network

3.12 Additional SAP Components

In addition to the AS ABAP–related kernel, other components could be in use too, but this depends on the individual solution. When defining an appropriate monitoring concept for these components you should ask yourself the following questions:

- How important is the availability of the component for the availability of my business processes?
- Which performance criteria does the component have to meet so as not to affect my business processes?
- Which technical details of the component help me draw conclusions about the status of my business processes?
- To what extent do certain monitoring objects of a component affect my business processes?
- What measures can be taken for the individual monitoring objects in case of an alarm?

3.12.1 liveCache Operating Status

Let's take a look at the SAP Advanced Planner and Optimizer (APO) example of our enterprise, Toys Inc.

In addition to the APO database, a liveCache has to be part of the system. If the liveCache fails, the APO system will no longer function. Therefore, the availability of the liveCache is as important as that of the APO database. Hence, the availability of the liveCache (see Table 3.36) is a very important monitoring object.

Category	liveCache
Monitoring object	Status
Monitoring attribute of the object	Current operating status of liveCache kernel process
Responsibility	Centralized system monitoring
Type of monitoring	Automated
Autoreaction method	Yes

Table 3.36 Monitoring the liveCache Status

Depending on the business process, the APO solution can be operated with or without an optimizer. They are only important if you use optimizers in your business processes. Thus, it depends on your business processes whether or not you need a monitoring object for the availability of the optimizers. In the sample scenario with Toys Inc. we don't use any optimizers.

3.12.2 liveCache Memory Management and Data Backup

SAP liveCache is a type of database instance based on SAP's MaxDB technology. Like every other database, liveCache contains technical components that are needed to ensure backup and stability. For example, to avoid a liveCache standstill due to completely full log volumes you have to perform a log backup — provided that there is at least one complete data backup of this database available. Therefore, it is recommended to run a daily backup.

To avoid a liveCache standstill you have to monitor both the freely available data area and the log area. It is very important to monitor the last data backup (see Tables 3.37 and 3.38) because this is the only way to avoid a loss of data if it has to be recovered due to hardware or software problems.

Category	liveCache
Monitoring object	Memory management
Monitoring attribute I of the object	Used data area of data volumes
Monitoring attribute II of the object	Used log area of log volumes
Monitoring attribute III of the object	Status of automatic log backup
Responsibility	Centralized system monitoring
Type of monitoring	Automated
Autoreaction method	No

Table 3.37 Monitoring the liveCache Memory Management

Certain performance-relevant criteria enable you to better understand the current status of your system. Not only does a slow system demotivate users, it can also lead to a system breakdown, which would have a substantial effect on business processes. Consequently, the required throughput cannot be reached anymore or users have to work overtime. This could even result in financial losses for the enterprise.

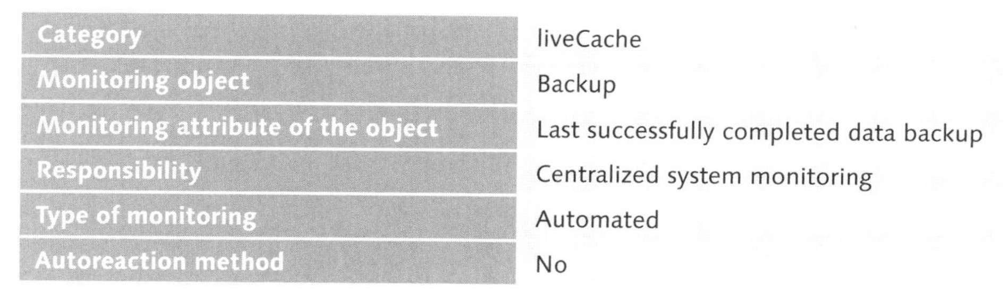

Category	liveCache
Monitoring object	Backup
Monitoring attribute of the object	Last successfully completed data backup
Responsibility	Centralized system monitoring
Type of monitoring	Automated
Autoreaction method	No

Table 3.38 Monitoring the liveCache Backup Runs

3.13 Database

The world of IT today is not conceivable without the use of Database Management Systems (DBMS). Without a DBMS it wouldn't be possible to master the vast amount of data that has to be processed and evaluated. To ensure availability, database integrity and performance, redundancy and data security, it is necessary to implement regular database monitoring.

If you monitor the database regularly you'll get information about the database during operation; you will be notified about problems and can prevent critical situations by using proactive measures. In addition, you will be able to identify and analyze problems and gather the necessary information about the settings of the database system. To monitor a DBMS you should include indicators such as the database size, the quality of the database buffers, possible storage space problems, and database performance.

There are various providers of database systems on the market, and each DBMS is based on a database model. We usually distinguish between hierarchical, relational, and object-oriented database models. Regardless of the type of database model you use you can specify a general approach for monitoring a DBMS. Therefore, the following sections discuss the monitoring objects that are common to all database systems and that we can apply to our sample enterprise.

3.13.1 Database and Table Growth

Database growth assumes a central role in today's system landscapes. In every business process, information forms the basis of actions and decisions. Today, decisions are increasingly made based on evaluations using evaluation tools, such as SAP NetWeaver BW. Accordingly, you must consider that the data volume has grown exponentially for some years now and that the new tools in a system landscape require a higher amount of data. The maintenance effort increases together with the growing data volume — but despite increasing maintenance expenditures database access becomes more and more inefficient, which can have an impact on the performance of business processes that is eventually noticed by users. You can counteract all of these problems by implementing proactive measures, such as the regular control of the database growth.

One way to increase performance would be to implement better CPUs and a higher storage capacity to handle the continuously growing amount of data. However, the technical limits will be quickly reached. So it would be better to find out how you can decrease the database size. For example, you could archive, compress, or reorganize your data to reduce the size of the database. Tables 3.39 and 3.40 list the objects for the database and table size growth.

Category	Database
Monitoring object	Database
Monitoring attribute of the object	Size of database and its rate of growth
Responsibility	Centralized system monitoring
Type of monitoring	Automated
Autoreaction method	No

Table 3.39 Monitoring Database Growth

Category	Database
Monitoring object	Tables
Monitoring attribute of the object	Table size and growth
Responsibility	Centralized system monitoring
Type of monitoring	Automated
Autoreaction method	No

Table 3.40 Monitoring Table Growth

3.13.2 Database Buffers

Every database contains different buffers that are used to store both database management information and user data in the main memory. The use of buffers in the main memory reduces the number of accesses to the hard disk, which, in turn, shortens the access time for objects that are already in the buffer. I/O accesses should be avoided because every access to the hard disk slows down processing speed.

For database performance the access qualities to database buffers are much more relevant. Depending on the database system there are different threshold values your system shouldn't fall short of. In a MaxDB instance the database buffer hit ratio is 99% (see Table 3.41).

Category	Database
Monitoring object	Database buffer
Monitoring attribute of the object	Database buffer quality
Responsibility	Centralized system monitoring
Type of monitoring	Automated
Autoreaction method	No

Table 3.41 Monitoring the Database Buffer

3.13.3 Lock Entries (AC/D)

The lock concept for ABAP systems specifies that an object can only be locked for the duration of a dialog step. If an unplanned termination of a dialog step occurs before the command for removing a database lock can be sent, then unwanted object locks can occur. This should be determined at an early stage because a locked object generates an error in a new update process and then the updates cannot be completed. Therefore, it is recommended to monitor lock objects for the duration of the lock status to resolve objects that last beyond the duration of a dialog process (see Table 3.42).

Category	Database
Monitoring object	Lock entries
Monitoring attribute of the object	Duration of the lock status
Responsibility	Centralized system monitoring
Type of monitoring	Automated
Autoreaction method	Yes

Table 3.42 Monitoring the Lock Entries

3.13.4 I/O Activities — Hard Disk Accesses

For optimal performance you must ensure equal loads for each hard disk of the database. If some of the hard disks are exposed to higher loads, an indicator of which is a higher hard disk utilization, an I/O bottleneck could result. This means longer wait and response times for I/O operations on the highly frequented disks. You can avoid I/O bottlenecks by better distributing the data to all of the disks in your system (see Table 3.43).

Category	Database
Monitoring object	Hard disks
Monitoring attribute of the object	Wait and response times of I/O operations
Responsibility	Centralized system monitoring
Type of monitoring	Automated
Autoreaction method	No

Table 3.43 Monitoring I/O Activities

3.13.5 Database Structure Check

To use data, it is important that you can trust that the entries to the database are processed safely and directly. An influencing factor is the consistency of data. If the records have an inconsistent state, no transaction on these datasets will result in a successful update. The reason for this is a property that is also incorporated in the Atomicity, Consistency, Isolation, and Durability (ACID) principle. This principle says that you can only update data records that come from a consistent state and may be transferred to such a state again during a transaction. To keep a consistent database, a weekly background process checks for compliance. Therefore, it is important to ensure that this background process runs successfully. The background process checks the structural consistency of the dataset in the database, but not the consistency of the content (see Table 3.44).

Category	Database
Monitoring object	Consistency check
Monitoring attribute of the object	Time until the last successful consistency check
Responsibility	Centralized system monitoring
Type of monitoring	Automated
Autoreaction method	No

Table 3.44 Monitoring Data Consistency

3.13.6 Data Backup

One of the major tasks of a system administrator is to ensure that data is continuously backed up. By running regular backups you can minimize the impact of hardware defects, damages caused by force majeure, or even the loss of data due to unintentional delete or overwrite processes. Basically, a data backup is the only way to recover data, and you will not be able to see how useful it is until the very moment when you have to recover lost data.

To avoid a loss of data and to increase the probability that the current data can actually be recovered, it is important that you monitor the data backup process. For example, if you have to perform a data recovery and during the recovery process you notice that the last successful backup was more than a week ago, your data is no longer up to date. All of the changes to data that have been done after the last successful backup can only be recovered via the log entries. This process is extremely time consuming and presumes the availability of the logs (see Table 3.45).

Category	Database
Monitoring object	Data backup
Monitoring attribute of the object	Last successfully completed data backup
Responsibility	Centralized system monitoring
Type of monitoring	Automated
Autoreaction method	No

Table 3.45 Monitoring the Data Backup

3.14 Communication Interfaces

The exchange of data between two SAP systems, an SAP system and a third-party system, or two third-party systems happens through a communication interface. For example, a data exchange takes place if an availability check is performed in the supplier system due to a customer request concerning a specific material; a data exchange also takes place when order confirmations, delivery notes, or invoices are sent to customers. It doesn't matter if the data transfer is synchronous or asynchronous, it must be transferred properly and orders arriving in the target system must be processed correctly.

To ensure a smooth data exchange you need specific information for your monitoring processes depending on the communication technology you use (for instance, RFC, IDoc, Business Application Programming Interface (BAPI)). This means it is necessary to become familiar with communication technology in general to decide which monitoring objects to include in the monitoring process.

In the system monitoring of our sample enterprise, Toys Inc., the transactional RFC (tRFC) and the qRFC play an important role. Both the transactional and the queued RFCs are variants of the RFCs that are used to make data transfers between different SAP systems more reliable and secure.

3.14.1 tRFC

The transfer of data between separate SAP systems or an SAP system and an external component is enabled by the tRFC function. The same ACID rules apply for tRFCs as for the database transactions:

- **Atomicity**
  If an error occurs during a transaction, all changes done to the database until this moment are undone. This means either all of the changes that a transaction does to a database are applied or none of them.
- **Consistency**
  All integrity conditions of the database are adhered to. That is to say, on the basis of a consistent status of the database the result of any transaction also has to be a consistent database status.
- **Isolation**
  Every transaction runs isolated from other transactions and doesn't depend on

others. This also implies that for each transaction the database only makes data available that is part of a consistent state.

- **Durability**
  It is ensured that after a successful commit, changes are stored in the database.

This means that every data block sent to the target system is transferred and processed completely or not at all. If an error occurs, the action is rolled back so that a consistent state is reached. Although tRFC does increase the reliability of data transfers substantially, it also contains some drawbacks. For example, it cannot be guaranteed that the sequence of Logical Units of Work (LUWs) specified in an application will be adhered to. It can only be guaranteed that all LUWs will be transferred sooner or later.

During a transfer, different error statuses can occur. A typical example of this is a network or communication problem that occurs during the transfer of an LUW. This error status can be identified by the CPICERR error message. If the system returns the SYSFAIL error message, it means that a serious error occurred in the target system during the processing of the LUW, which will then terminate. If the sending system tries to send an LUW directly without using any outbound queues and there's no free work process available, the system will return the SYSLOAD error message (see Table 3.46).

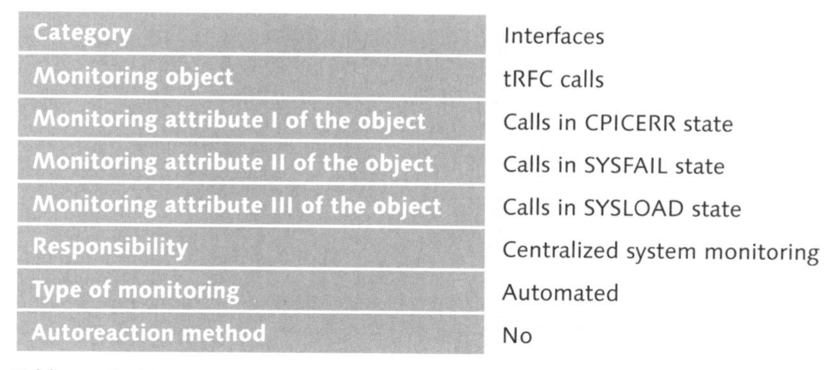

Category	Interfaces
Monitoring object	tRFC calls
Monitoring attribute I of the object	Calls in CPICERR state
Monitoring attribute II of the object	Calls in SYSFAIL state
Monitoring attribute III of the object	Calls in SYSLOAD state
Responsibility	Centralized system monitoring
Type of monitoring	Automated
Autoreaction method	No

Table 3.46 Monitoring tRFC

3.14.2 qRFC

To counteract the nonserial and unsorted transfer of tRFC a serialization of tRFC takes place via queues, which is called qRFC. qRFC is an enhancement of tRFC and it groups tRFC calls into outbound and inbound queues. If you use qRFC with outbound queues (see Table 3.47) you can make sure that tRFC calls will be executed in the target system in exactly the same sequence as they were added to the queue.

Category	Interfaces
Monitoring object	qRFC outbound queues
Monitoring attribute of the object	Status of the queue
Responsibility	Centralized system monitoring
Type of monitoring	Automated
Autoreaction method	No

Table 3.47 Monitoring qRFC Outbound Queues

If you use qRFC with inbound queues (see Table 3.48) you can make sure that incoming calls for a specific queue will be executed in the sequence in which they arrive. qRFC is used particularly in the *Core Interface* (CIF) for data transfers between SCM and ERP systems (ABAP).

Whether a transmission request is processed successfully is monitored in both the outbound and inbound queues (see Table 3.48).

Category	Interfaces
Monitoring object	qRFC inbound queues
Monitoring attribute of the object	Status of the queue
Responsibility	Centralized system monitoring
Type of monitoring	Automated
Autoreaction method	No

Table 3.48 Monitoring qRFC Inbound Queues

3.14.3 QIN and QOUT Scheduler

On the basis of currently existing system resources the QIN Scheduler has to activate as many inbound queues as possible. It only includes queues that are registered. In addition, the QIN Scheduler can monitor the runtime of a queue at the end of an LUW execution to hold it up, if necessary, so that other queues can be processed as well. The QIN Scheduler controls the processing of incoming tRFC and qRFC calls within a specific client.

To avoid overloading the target system with too many transmission requests you can use the QOUT Scheduler. This tool helps you limit the maximum number of parallel connections (tRFC/qRFC) for a specific connection so that the maximum number of RFCs can be controlled. It is recommended that you monitor the status of the QOUT Scheduler.

Your system monitoring model should include a regular check of the status of the QIN and QOUT Schedulers. They control and monitor an equal distribution of RFC resources, which enables you to avoid resource and performance problems in an SAP system (see Tables 3.49 and 3.50).

Category	Interfaces
Monitoring object	QIN Scheduler
Monitoring attribute of the object	Inbound scheduler error
Responsibility	Centralized system monitoring
Type of monitoring	Automated
Autoreaction method	No

Table 3.49 Monitoring the QIN Scheduler

Category	Interfaces
Monitoring object	QOUT Scheduler
Monitoring attribute of the object	Outbound scheduler error
Responsibility	Centralized system monitoring
Type of monitoring	Automated
Autoreaction method	No

Table 3.50 Monitoring the QOUT Scheduler

3.15 BW Process Chain Monitoring

Due to the growing demand for aggregated information, it is important to monitor the process of creating such data and the reports that are based on it. Toys Inc. has created a multitude of evaluation reports to support management and provided them in an internal portal for use. For Toys Inc. it is important to evaluate and present trend analyses with regard to sales — but also the stock development based on current figures. To do this, Toys Inc. hired a consultant in the last business year who prepared reports and created the process chains for automated extraction, aggregation, and transfer to the evaluation system (BW). These process chains are primarily executed in a background process at night. Toys Inc. faces the challenge to automatically monitor the error-free execution of all process chains.

The status of the process chains is to be included in the monitoring. If a process chain is only implemented in parts or not at all due to performance, authorization, or resource reasons, this is indicated in a status that can be used in the monitoring for the analyses (see Table 3.51).

Category	BW
Monitoring object	Process chains
Monitoring attribute of the object	Status process chains
Responsibility	Centralized system monitoring
Type of monitoring	Automated
Autoreaction method	No

Table 3.51 Monitoring the Status of Process Chains

Notes on Considering the BW System in Monitoring

A BW system is managed separately and considered separately in system monitoring. The BW system is primarily a system in which you generate and process information. This main task of the system is not subject to the same requirements regarding the dialog response time like an ERP system, for example.

The activities of information processing are frequently implemented in times with low loads to avoid unnecessary loads during productive working times of an enterprise. This way, you can provide information without larger loads during productive time. The generation of all of the information required and the generation of information outside the productive time should be monitored using system monitoring to determine disruptions in information processing in good time or to respond to disruptions quickly.

From the determined objects, Toys Inc. specified the following objects as relevant to the BW system:

- Background processing
  - Process chains
  - Reorganization processes
- Interface monitoring
- Availability of the ABAP instance and the availability of the Web presence (including the results)
- Database monitoring
  - Memory utilization
  - Consistency
  - Optimization

3.16 Self-Monitoring of Monitoring Tools

To ensure the proper operation of your systems it is not only necessary to monitor the individual components of your system landscape but also the monitoring tools themselves have to be checked regularly to see if they run properly. If they don't function there can be no automated monitoring.

Because SAP Solution Manager is the monitoring tool used in our example the following sections describe certain criteria related to this tool. In addition, you will find information about some areas that you have to consider as prerequisites if you want to use SAP Solution Manager.

3.16.1 Availability of SAP Solution Manager Systems

You need to ensure the accessibility and availability of the centralized monitoring system (see Table 3.52). Therefore, when designing your monitoring concept, you must answer the following questions:

- How do you want to monitor the centralized monitoring system?
- Which monitoring objects and attributes have to be included in the monitoring process?
- Which monitoring procedures are activated if there is a failure of the monitoring tool?

As with all of the other SAP components you could configure availability monitoring via system availability and application server availability. This can be done using the availability agent CCMSPING.

You can find information about installing and configuring the CCMSPING agent in the SAP Service Marketplace by following the menu path: MONITORING • SYSTEM MONITORING AND ALERT MANAGEMENT • MEDIA LIBRARY • DOCUMENTATION • AVAILABILITY MONITORING AND AGENT CCMSPING.

Category	SAP Solution Manager
Monitoring object I	System availability
Monitoring object II	Instance availability
Monitoring attribute of the object I	Availability per system
Monitoring attribute of the object II	Status of instance availability
Responsibility	Centralized system monitoring
Type of monitoring	Automated
Autoreaction method	Yes

Table 3.52 Monitoring System and Instance Availability of SAP Solution Manager

3.16.2 Monitoring the Computing Center Management System (CCMS) Monitoring Architecture

The monitoring architecture of the CCMS provides an infrastructure to gather and manage system information. For the system monitoring process SAP Solution Manager uses functions of this monitoring architecture, which means that without the monitoring architecture SAP Solution Manager is not functional at all.

To collect data for different monitoring objects, data collectors are available that send data for monitored objects to the monitoring architecture. The monitoring architecture constantly compares the measurement values provided by the data collectors with the threshold values and triggers an alarm when the measurement values are above or below the thresholds. If the data collectors don't function properly, monitoring is not possible. For this reason, the data collectors themselves must also be monitored (see Table 3.53).

Category	Monitoring architecture
Monitoring object	Data collectors
Monitoring attribute of the object	Information about possible data collector problems
Responsibility	Centralized system monitoring
Type of monitoring	Automated
Autoreaction method	Yes

Table 3.53 Monitoring the Data Collectors

3.16.3 CCMS Agents

CCMS agents are self-contained processes that have an RFC interface to a central monitoring system and one to the shared memory. CCMS agents enable you to include SAP components that don't have an ABAP interface into your monitoring system.

CCMSs can collect monitoring data about the system, send this data to the central monitoring system, and save it in a cache for a faster display or to trigger a central autoresponse method.

If the central system doesn't have to request monitoring data from the monitored system on a regular basis, but an agent transfers this data to the central monitoring system, then this technology is called *push technology*. To use this technology a kernel release of at least SAP Web AS 6.10 or higher has to be installed in the centralized monitoring system, whose performance will improve substantially.

Depending on the type of system you want to monitor you can use the agents described in Table 3.54.

Agent	Task
SAPCCMSR	Monitoring components on which no AS ABAP instance is active
SAPCCM4X	Monitoring AS ABAP systems — Basis Release 4.x
SMD Agent	Infrastructural component of SAP Solution Manager Diagnostics implements the communication and transport of information between SAP Solution Manager and the system to be monitored
Introscope Agent	Determination of performance information in Java systems

Table 3.54 Agents in SAP Monitoring Landscapes

This book doesn't describe how to install, register, and use the agents, but you can find detailed documentation in the SAP Service Marketplace using the menu path: MONITORING • SYSTEM MONITORING AND ALERT MANAGEMENT • MONITORING IN DETAIL • CCMS AGENTS PROPERTIES, INSTALLATION AND OPERATION. The necessary information for the agents of the Solution Manager Diagnostics landscape is available in the SAP Service Marketplace via the path: DIAGNOSTICS • INSTALLATION AND CONFIGURATION.

3.16.4 SAPCCMSR

The SAPCCMSR agent monitors both SAP and non-SAP components where no SAP instance is active, such as databases without SAP instance or OS components.

The SAPCCMSR agent is used to incorporate SAP NetWeaver Portal and the non-SAP solution WAMA in the monitoring landscape. This agent enables communication between the different technologies of the monitoring system and the system to be monitored. It also lets SAP data collectors provide information via the satellite systems.

3.16.5 SAPCCM4X

You can use the SAPCCM4X agent to monitor SAP systems of Release 4.x or higher. This agent provides an alternative connection path for monitoring information about an SAP instance in shared memory. In this context, no free work process is needed to read and write the monitoring information, which means that monitoring data can be collected regardless of the status of the SAP instance.

What happens if the agent is inactive and unable to send data to the centralized monitoring system?

The centralized monitoring system will at first automatically attempt to read the data of the system being monitored through the RFC connection of the CCMS agent. If the agent is not active, the monitoring data of the SAP instance being monitored is read by the standard RFC as before.

The SAPCCM4X agent technology is used for the ECC system and the BW system. This technology is used to utilize the push technology described previously. This means the monitoring data is sent from the agents to the centralized monitoring system and the centralized monitoring system performance is ensured.

3.16.6 SMD Agent

The SMD agent establishes the communication bridge between SAP Solution Manager Diagnostics and the SAP system to be monitored. The basis of the SAP system to be monitored is not important here. The SMD agent is installed on the system to be monitored as an independent Java process and — as a representative of the system — ensures the communication with Solution Manager Diagnostics. If the agent is not available, no failure scenario exists and the data cannot be collected as of the point in time when the connection was interrupted. Monitoring the agent is only possible manually at the current status of technical developments. Future versions of SAP Solution Manager are supposed to provide a comprehensive option for monitoring SMD agents.

3.16.7 Introscope Agent

The Wily Introscope agent is used to gather performance information of Java, C#, and .NET applications. The information is recorded in real time and provided in Wily Enterprise Manager for product-specific aggregation and preparation. It is collected by the BW system at hourly intervals and provided to the End-to-End Root Cause Analysis tools.

The technical integration and implementation of Wily Introscope components is not further discussed in this book; for this reason, the SAP Service Marketplace provides the Master Implementation Guide (IMG) under the DIAGNOSTICS quick link. Currently, SAP doesn't provide any standards for the monitoring of the agent. These standards are supposed to be an integral part of the next deliveries of SAP Solution Manager. Based on the current technological status it is recommended to manually check the agent at regular intervals. If the agent is not available, no data is collected and written to the monitored system (see Table 3.55).

Category	CCMS agents
Monitoring object I	SAPCCMSR
Monitoring object II	SAPCCM4X
Monitoring attribute of objects I and II	Availability
Responsibility	Centralized system monitoring
Type of monitoring	Automated
Autoreaction method	Yes

Table 3.55 Monitoring the CCMS Agents

3.17 Monitoring System Components Without an SAP Instance

Components outside the SAP environment must also be monitored. Some manufacturers provide an individual monitoring tool compatible with their application. The advantage of this is that these tools are generally available for immediate use with little difficulty. The disadvantage, however, is that the centralized monitoring function becomes irrelevant during the simultaneous use of several monitoring tools in a heterogeneous system environment. A useful solution is the provision of a central monitoring tool to send monitoring data from non-SAP components to the centralized monitoring tool via interfaces.

SAP also provides tools to monitor non-SAP components. The SAPCCMSR agent is one of these. This agent monitors components that have no active SAP instance. It compiles data and sends it to the centralized monitoring system. Log files, independent databases along with their components, or OS components, for example, can be integrated into the monitoring process. To do this, Toys Inc. can use SAPCCMSR agents and, if necessary, develop further interfaces.

3.17.1 Log File

It is possible to monitor log files from SAP and non-SAP components. Monitoring is carried out through the SAPCCMSR CCMS agent in components that are not part of the SAP environment. A log file agent is integrated into these agents and other SAP CCMS agents and it monitors log files according to specific search patterns. This means searches can be carried out in any text file for any text sample. These can be assigned alerts and the results can be displayed in the alert monitor using the suitable text pattern (see Table 3.56).

Category	Log file
Monitoring object	<Name of the log file>
Monitoring attribute of the object	<Search pattern>
Responsibility	Centralized system monitoring
Type of monitoring	Automated
Autoreaction method	No

Table 3.56 Monitoring Log Files

The following log file types can be monitored by CCMS agents:

- Log files that are continuously described by the application and therefore constantly increase
- Log files that are rewritten by the application after each restart under the same names
- Log files that are created every time by the application with new names

3.17.2 OS

Monitoring the OSs of non-SAP systems is another focal point. Depending on the monitoring objects, which were described in Section 3.2, Operating System (OS), these objects must also be taken into consideration in system components outside of the SAP environment in the monitoring process. The SAPCCMSR CCMS agent in combination with SAPOSCOL is also used for this. After a successful installation of the two agents, the OS Collector provides the OS information as usual and transfers it to the memory area, which is managed by the SAPCCMSR agent. The SAPCCMSR agent provides this information in the monitoring system using the described push technology (see Section 3.16.3, CCMS Agents). There, the information is displayed in the CCMS monitoring architecture.

3.18 Documenting Changes in System Monitoring

The previous sections described the content of the monitoring concept. You have learned about the typical components of a monitoring concept. The issue of how the process looks if changes are made in the monitoring still remains to be discussed. For example, you can integrate new monitoring objects into the monitoring process or threshold values for a monitoring object may still need to be adapted, or the troubleshooting procedure for an object has changed. As you can see, there are countless reasons why a change could become necessary.

Change logs in system monitoring are important if an outsourcer takes over monitoring the system landscape. SLAs on system maintenance are generally agreed upon at the beginning of a business relationship between the outsourcer and the customer. They form the basis for establishing the criteria that can play a role in system monitoring. If it emerges after production begins that the criteria established do not 100% fulfill the agreements, the criteria must be revised.

Errors can also occur in the adaptation process. They can be found and traced more easily by using documentation.

3.18.1 Responsibility for the Documentation

To avoid individuals making changes to the system monitoring at will, it is of critical importance to appoint an administrator. Suggested changes are notified to this person. With expert support they will decide whether or not to implement these changes.

3.18.2 Change Log

A change log must be simple and straightforward. You should include the following information in the documentation:

- the reason for the change and a brief description
- the individual(s) who made the suggestion
- the individual(s) who supported the administrator in making the decision
- the implementation process effort
- the effects of the changes when introduced
- the date for adapting it in system monitoring
- the individual who will carry out the customization in the monitoring system

3.18.3 Process Description

An essential point is the creation of a process description. This should contain a procedure for making changes in the system monitoring model. When the centralized monitoring system has just been newly introduced, due to initial experiences on a technical and organizational level, changes will almost certainly be necessary. The definition of suitable threshold values is an iterative process that is based on experience. Upon completion ensure that individuals involved in system monitoring are aware of the changes made to the process to maintain a consistent and complete status of the system monitoring in the monitoring concept.

4 System Monitoring Using SAP Solution Manager 7.0

This chapter provides an overview of how to set up and use SAP Solution Manager 7.0 and its components for system monitoring. It covers Computing Center Management System (CCMS) and SAP Solution Manager Diagnostics. You will learn the technical prerequisites for the central monitoring system and for the monitored systems. Then we'll look at the SAP Solution Manager configuration and the system monitoring implementation process. The implementation process for the central autoreaction method in the central monitoring system is also discussed.

4.1 Technological Delimitation

As already described in Chapter 2, Section 2.2, Scenarios of SAP Solution Manager, SAP Solution Manager 7.0 is made up of several components. Some of these components are also used in system monitoring. The CCMS serves as a basis of system monitoring in SAP Solution Manager, and the End-to-End Root Cause Analysis tools make up the system monitoring for the entire information technology (IT) landscape.

4.1.1 CCMS

The monitoring architecture of the CCMS provides every AS ABAP system with a flexible and globally usable infrastructure that monitors the entire SAP system landscape and provides fast, reliable reports on any problems that occur. SAP Solution Manager monitoring techniques are based on CCMS functions. Its functions include monitoring the hardware, database, SAP basis components, availability monitoring, and analysis and data collection methods. This means that SAP Solution Manager cannot function as a monitoring tool without CCMS monitoring architecture.

4.1.2 End-to-End Workload Analysis

The End-To-End Workload Analysis is a tool of Solution Manager Diagnostics. It provides a performance analysis of IT landscapes across system boundaries and considers the entire execution process of a query that was made by a user in an IT landscape. It measures the lead times for all technical components that are involved in the execution process. Release SR4 of SAP Solution Manager, which is still up to date, does not let you integrate systems without ABAP basis with central monitoring to monitor the performance of the systems. Therefore, you use workload analysis information for system monitoring of non-ABAP systems. Particularly in solution landscapes that use different technologies, such as AS Java and ABAP, .NET or C++, the End-to-End Workload Analysis simplifies the Root Cause Analysis to a large extent when performance problems occur.

4.2 Prerequisites

Before system monitoring can be set up in SAP Solution Manager we need to know which general activities and prerequisites are necessary for the implementation process. For a few additional monitoring objects some more prerequisites are needed. For example, for availability monitoring you also need CCMSPING agents. Reference is made to specific prerequisites for these and other monitoring objects during the implementation processes in the corresponding sections. You also need to implement Solution Manager Diagnostics to obtain performance information on all of the systems. The following sections refer to the different administrative steps and installations that are necessary for implementation in the Solution Manager system and in the systems that are supposed to be monitored.

Term Definition: Satellite Systems

Systems connected to the SAP Solution Manager, which are monitored, are called *satellite systems* or *managed systems*. Throughout this chapter, we use the term "satellite system."

4.2.1 Installing SAP Solution Manager

The first step to a SAP Solution Manager production system that functions as a monitoring tool is the installation of SAP Solution Manager 7.0. You can find the document for the installation in the SAP Service Marketplace. You can download it by following the menu path: SAP COMPONENTS • SAP SOLUTION MANAGER • RELEASE 7.0 • INSTALLATION GUIDES. SAP Solution Manager is usually operated as a *double stack*, that is, an installation that consists of AS ABAP and AS Java.

Depending on which operating system (OS) and database SAP Solution Manager will run on, choose the corresponding installation manual. Figure 4.1 gives you an overview of the current installation documents for SAP Solution Manager in the SAP Service Marketplace. Carry out the individual steps according to this document. This book does not go into further detail on installing SAP Solution Manager 7.0.

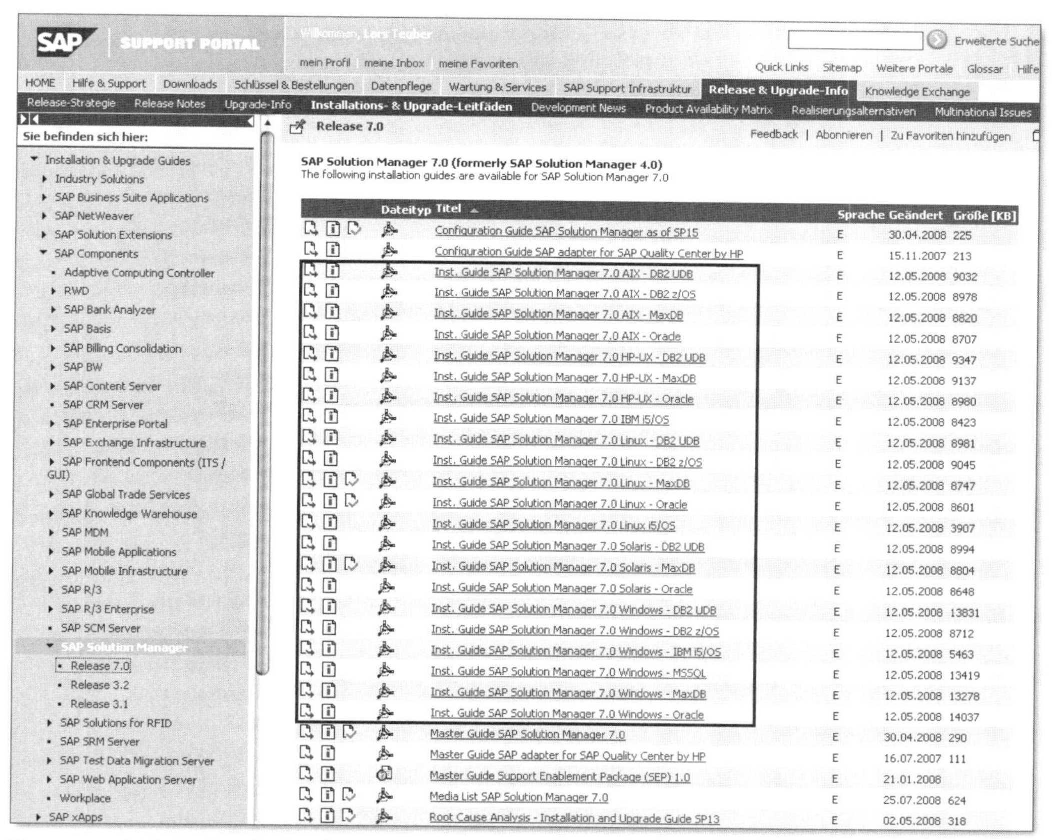

Figure 4.1 SAP Service Marketplace — Overview of the SAP Solution Manager Installation Documents

4.2.2 Support Packages

If you use SAP Solution Manager 7.0, including the End-to-End Root Cause Analysis tools, you need the support packages from Table 4.1 and the SP level statuses listed.

It is recommended to install the latest support package, which contains corrections and upgrades. Table 4.1 provides an overview of the SAP Solution Manager used for Toys Inc.

4.2.3 Components of SAP Solution Manager 7.0

SAP delivers SAP Solution Manager in Product Version 7.0 as a stand-alone installation. Software Release 4 contains the current delivery media, which provides SAP Solution Manager in Support Package Stack 13. You can find the support packages for updating SAP Solution Manager 7.0 in the SAP Service Marketplace under the following menu path: PATCHES • ENTRY BY APPLICATION GROUP • SAP TECHNOLOGY COMPONENTS • SAP SOLUTION MANAGER • SAP SOLUTION MANAGER 7.0 (see Figure 4.2).

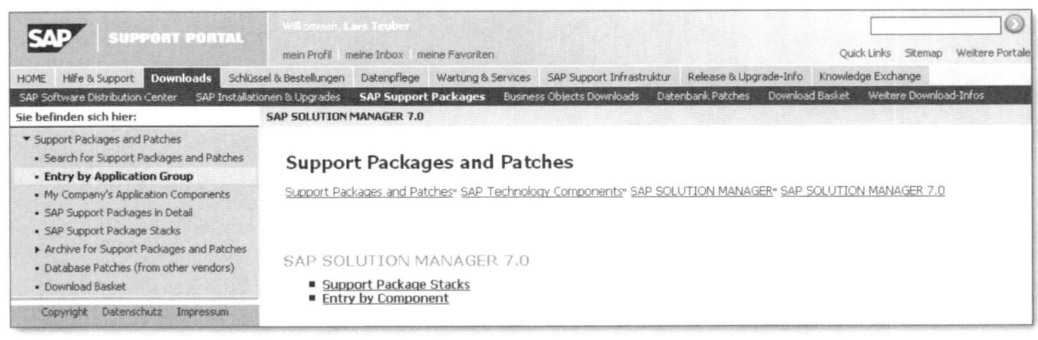

Figure 4.2 SAP Service Marketplace — Download of Support Packages for SAP Solution Manager 7.0

Since April 1, 2007, the provision of the support packages for SAP NetWeaver 7.0 and SAP Business Suite 2005 from the SAP Service Marketplace is mapped as a process in SAP Solution Manager via the Maintenance Optimizer (MOPZ), which also supports the implementation. For more information on the Maintenance Optimizer, please visit the SAP Service Marketplace: *service.sap.com/solman-mopz*. For the first installation, you should configure SAP Solution Manager in the standard delivery and immediately activate the MOPZ. This enables you to use MOPZ with recent support packages from the SAP Service Marketplace and upgrade SAP Solution Manager to the latest release.

Further add-ons (components) are available depending on the functionalities that are used in SAP Solution Manager. Some of these are explained in the following sections. Please note that add-on installations can only be installed on components of specific releases.

ST-PI — SAP Solution Tools Plug-In

ST-PI contains the latest versions of the following functions:

- Data collection elements
- Transaction SDCCN (Service Data Control Center)
- Transaction SQLR (SQL Trace Interpreter)
- Function modules that use Transaction SMSY to read system information

SDCCN and SQLR are contained in ST-PI for SAP Release 4.0B to 4.6D. Since Release 6.10 of SAP Web Application Server (WAS), the transactions are contained in SAP Basis Standard. Corrections and new versions are supplied in Basis support packages.

ST-ICO — SAP Solution Manager Implementation Content

The ST-ICO add-on provides content, which is used in SAP Solution Manager, to implement SAP solutions. These are descriptions and integrated configuration information for business scenarios that are supported by SAP and product-specific information for projects being implemented, in operation, and for upgrading an SAP system landscape, sorted according to the usual phases of such projects.

ST-SER — SAP Solution Services

The ST-SER add-on provides content that is used in SAP Solution Manager to implement, operate, and monitor SAP solutions.

ST-A/PI — Application Service Tools

The ST-A/PI add-on contains application-specific tools, the ST14 application monitor, and the RTCCTOOL report. These must be installed in preparation of an SAP service, such as the SAP EarlyWatch Check. From Release 4.0B on, SAP systems contain these application-specific tools in ST-A/PI. ST14 and RTCCTOOL are only supplied as separate Sapserv 3-7 transports with the older R/3 3.0D-3.1I releases.

PI_Basis — SAP Basis Plug-In

The SAP Basis Plug-in is a software component that can be installed on an SAP WAS or any other product that runs on SAP_BASIS 700 or SAP_ABA 700 or higher. It facilitates communication between different application systems that run on different platforms. Note that the SAP Basis Plug-in requires the AS-ABAP Plug-in. That means that when you upgrade the AS-ABAP Plug-in, SAP Basis Plug-in must also be upgraded.

SAP Solution Manager, Enterprise Edition

The enterprise edition of SAP Solution Manager enables you to use enterprise support services. You can only activate and use the following enhancements in SAP Solution Manager if you have a valid support contract. For more information on licenses and use, contact the contracts departments of your subsidiary. The following enhancements are part of the SAP Solution Manager, enterprise edition:

- **SAP Adapter for Quality Center by HP — ST-QCA**
  SAP Quality Center by HP enables you to process business testing requirements (blueprints) and transfers them to the quality center for organizing the tests.
- **SAP Process Scheduling Adapter — ST-PSM**
  PSM provides functions for locking and releasing structure nodes, tabs, and attributes in a project structure.
- **SAP NetWeaver Business Warehouse (BW)**
  Originally, SAP NetWeaver BW was delivered as a reporting tool in the SAP Business Warehouse (BW) package. The BI_CONT package provides the system with content, definitions, and structures. It contains, for example, the predefined InfoProviders, InfoCubes, and queries for performance reporting. Solution Manager Diagnostics maps information mainly on the basis of predefined queries of the BI_CONT package. Therefore, it is essential that this package is always up to date.

Table 4.1 lists the minimum support package level for using SAP Solution Manager 7.0:

Component	Package Name	Support Package Level
SAP Basis NetWeaver 7.0	SAP_BASIS	Release 700 Level 15
	SAP_ABA	Release 700 Level 15
	SAP_AP	Release 700 Level 12
SAP Solution Manager	ST	Release 400 Level 16
	ST-PI	Release 2005_1_700 Level 6
	ST-A/PI	Release 01K_CRM560
	ST-SER	Release 700_2008_1 Level 4
	ST-ICO	Release 150_700 Level 14
SAP NetWeaver BW	SAP_BW	Release 700 Level 17
	BI_CONT	Release 703 Level 10
SAP NetWeaver Process Integration	PI_BASIS	Release 2006_1_700 Level 6
SAP Customer Relationship Management (CRM)	BBPCRM	Release 500 Level 11
	CPRXRPM	Release 400 Level 11
SAP Enhancement Packages (Enterprise Edition)	ST-QCA	Release 100 Level 0
	ST-PSM	Release 100 Level 0
	ST-ETP	Release 100 Level 0

Table 4.1 Minimum Support Package Level for Using SAP Solution Manager 7.0

4.2.4 Components in Satellite Systems — ST-PI and ST-A/PI

Besides the requirements within SAP Solution Manager, you must also meet the specific requirements of the satellite systems that have to be managed. For monitoring satellite systems, two components are necessary. Use the latest version of ST-PI and ST-A/PI if you implement them in the satellite system and on SAP Solution Manager.

4.2.5 SAP Solution Manager System Users

You must create a user in your SAP Solution Manager system to maintain and manage it.

For the initial configuration, you should create a temporary user that is provided with comprehensive administrative authorizations in SAP Solution Manager. The initial configuration comprises the creation of users, Remote Function Call (RFC) connections, the set up of background processes and modifications in system tables. Table 4.2 shows a proposal for this temporary user that is required for the setup. Once the initial configuration is completed, the user should be deactivated.

User	Profiles
SOLMANINST	SAP_ALL
	SAP_NEW

Table 4.2 The SOLMANINST Temporary User and its SAP Solution Manager Profile

Furthermore, you should also create a user that you can use for additional administrative activities. For example, this user should be able to create solution landscapes and set up background processes.

Additional users, for example, for communication with satellite systems, are described with implementation later on.

Toys Inc. decided to use two additional users — one for administrative transactions in the dialog and one for the administration of periodical background processes. This decision is supposed to avoid problems with locked or inactive users. Table 4.3 shows an example of the authorizations for such users.

User	Type of User	Roles	Profiles
SOLMAN_BTC	Dialog	SAP_BC_BATCH_ADMIN	
SOLMAN_ADMIN	Dialog	SAP_SMWORK_BASIC	
		SAP_RFC_SM_CONFIG	
		SAP_SMWORK_BASIC	
		SAP_SMWORK_SYS_MON	

Table 4.3 Examples of Users and Their Roles and Profiles

To enable the communication between the systems, additional users may be required depending on the respective functional requirements.

4.2.6 Satellite System Users

For system monitoring, a user is needed to deliver monitoring data by remote access from the CCMS of the monitored systems to the SAP Solution Manager system. This user is automatically created when the systems that are supposed to be monitored are set up. However, this automated procedure is only possible if the systems that are supposed to be monitored are not linked to a central user administration. If this is the case, you must manually create the user in the satellite system (see Table 4.4)

User	Type of User	Roles	Profiles
SOLMAN<SID><CLNT>	Communication	SAP_Satellite_E2E	S_AI_SMD_E2E
			S_BDLSM_READ
			S_CSMREG
			S_CUS_CMP

Table 4.4 Users in the Satellite System and Their Authorizations

4.2.7 OS Collector — SAPOSCOL

The SAPOSCOL OS collector must be installed on each instance of a satellite system. It is an independent program that runs in the background. By default, SAPOSCOL collects current data on specific operating resources every ten seconds, for example memory usage and CPU and data system utilization. SAPOSCOL can be used in both SAP and non-SAP systems to monitor OS resources. You can find the latest version of SAPOSCOL in the SAP Service Marketplace.

4.3 SAP Solution Manager Configuration

This section shows you how to configure SAP Solution Manager to set up system monitoring later on.

4.3.1 Maintenance of the System Data

A system landscape contains several systems; each system, in turn, consists of hardware and software components. Each component has certain properties, for example, system data such as the number of CPUs on a host, or the status of a system's SAP Basis support package.

At this point, remember that you should first collect all of the relevant information on the systems and their components to create a concept before you begin with the configuration in SAP Solution Manager. This enables you to implement the configuration in one go as planned and without interruptions. In the case of Toys Inc., the required information on the monitoring concept was compiled in Chapter 3, Designing the Monitoring Concepts.

In SAP Solution Manager, you can read system data automatically, for example, from a directory or — in exceptional cases where a system is not maintained in a directory — transfer it manually to the system landscape.

- **Automatic data transfer of system data**
  Data can be automatically transferred from two different directories. The Transport Management System provides information on all systems that are contained in the transport domain. However, currently this does not include Java systems and refers only to the ABAP transport domain. An additional directory contains the *System Landscape Directory* (SLD). This Java-based directory lists all SAP system technologies and will be more important than ever in future strategies. Therefore, it should be considered in potential planning processes. The SLD retrieves its information from satellite systems by means of periodic transfer requests, which are background requests that send the system information to the SLD via the TCP/IP RFC connection. For Java systems, communication is defined via URLs. SAP Solution Manager can retrieve this information and map it in its own system directory (Transaction SMSY). If the automatic transfer is active, you cannot change system-relevant data manually — because this may lead to inconsistencies, this option is blocked by the system. You can only implement changes if the maintenance mode is not set to automatic data transfer. However, if you reset the mode to Automatic data transfer, the data will be overwritten again. If data isn't transferred correctly, you can only correct this at the source — the system or the SLD. Transaction SMSY_SETUP enables you to schedule automatic data transfers from directories (see Figure 4.3).

  This book does not deal with a system landscape setup and maintenance using automatic data transfers.

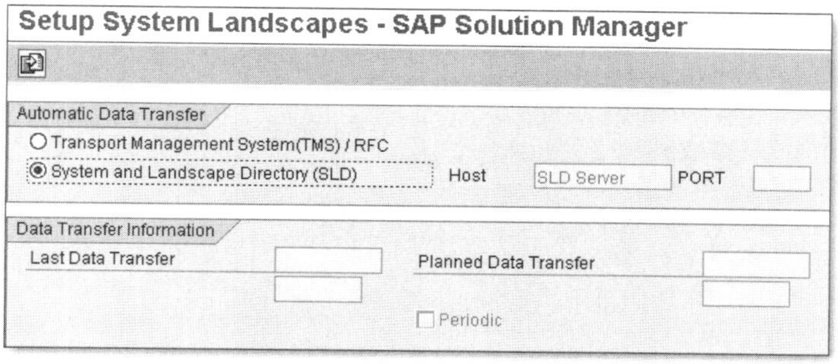

Figure 4.3 Setting up the Automatic System Transfer

- **Manual maintenance of the system data**
  The manual maintenance of the system comprises individual steps to manually create host data, database data, and system data for SAP and non-SAP systems.

  The following sections describe how you can include SAP systems with different kernel technologies and non-SAP systems in the directory. The ERP Central Component (ECC) 6.0 system with the System ID OTO is used to map the integration of the ABAP and Java components. To explain the additional steps that are required for non-SAP systems, the Warehouse Management (WAMA) system is used here. Let's start with the creation of SAP systems; note that for non-SAP systems the procedure as described in the following Product Definition of Non-SAP Products section is mandatory.

Creating Host Data

1. Call Transaction SMSY in your SAP Solution Manager.
2. Select the Server landscape component.
3. In the context menu (right-clicking on the Server landscape component), select Create New Server.
4. Enter the host name.
5. Save your entries.
6. Select the host name under the Hosts landscape component. On the right-hand side of the screen you can enter the details of the host. For End-to-End Root Cause Analysis tools, you must specify a value for the Fully Qualified Host Name parameter. Figure 4.4 illustrates the monitor used to create host data in Transaction SMSY.
7. Save your entries.

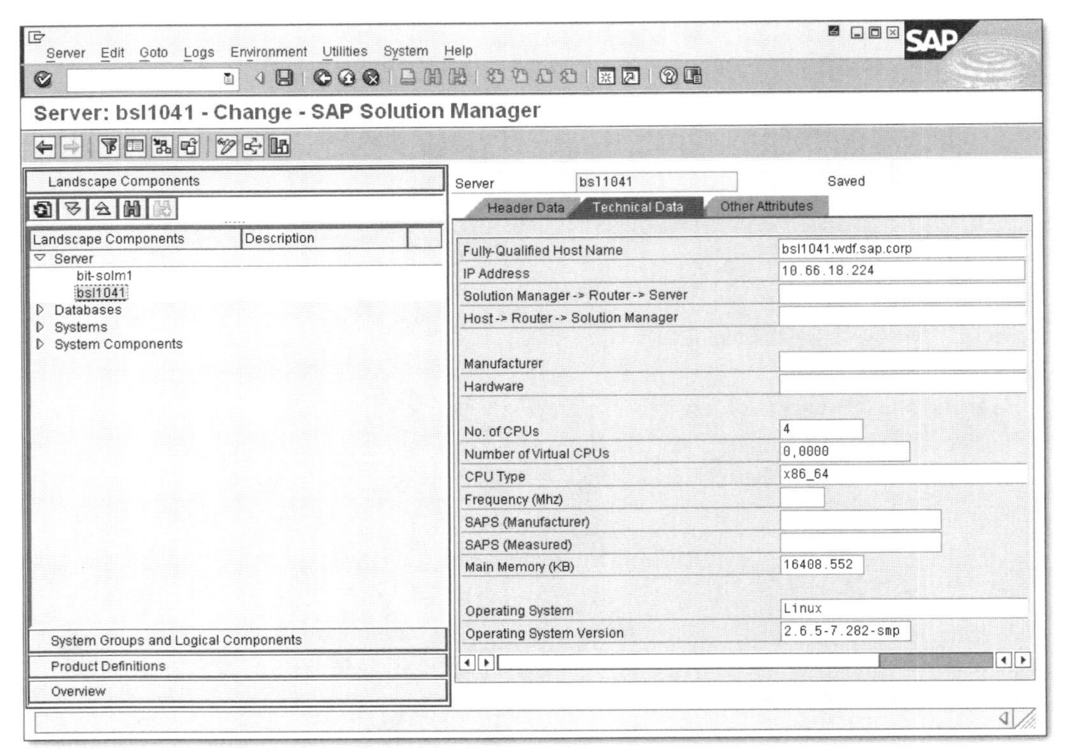

Figure 4.4 Creating Server Data

Creating Database Data

1. Call Transaction SMSY.
2. Select the Databases landscape component.
3. In the context menu (right-clicking on the Databases landscape component), select Create New Database.
4. Enter the database name.
5. Save your entries.
6. Select the database name under the Databases landscape component. On the right-hand side of the screen you can enter the database details. Figure 4.5 displays the monitor used to create databases data in Transaction SMSY.
7. Save your entries.

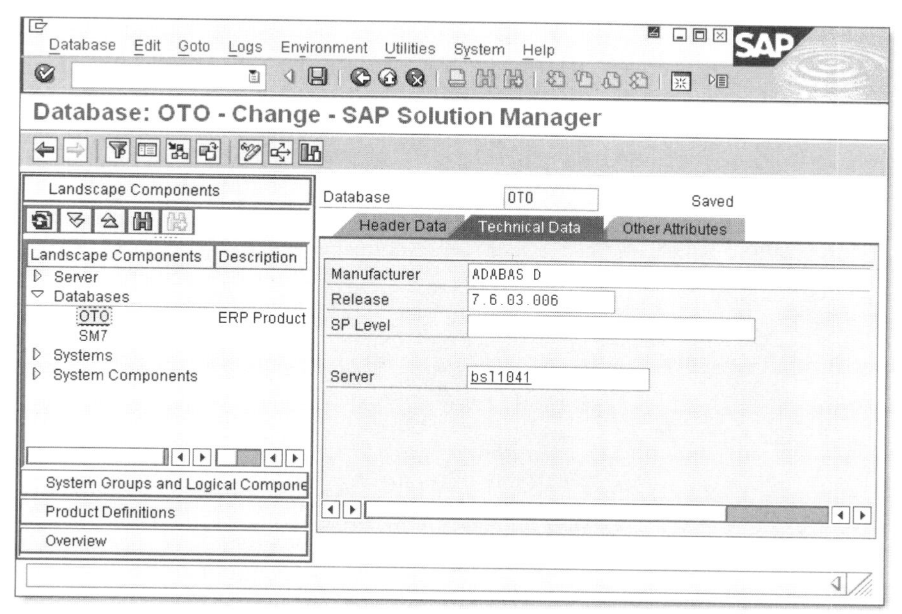

Figure 4.5 Creating Database for System OTO

Creating System Data

1. Call Transaction SMSY.
2. Select the Systems landscape component.
3. In the context menu (right-clicking on the Systems landscape component), select Create New System. Insert the system ID as a system name.
4. Select a product and a product version from the input help. If the product is not available, follow the instructions in the Product Definition of Non-SAP Products section.
5. Save your entries.
6. Select the System ID under the Systems • <Product> landscape component, and, if necessary, set a different ABAP-based main instance on the System Description tab to Relevant or set several non-ABAP main instances to Relevant. Only main instances marked as relevant can be displayed in the operational process in your solution landscape, as shown in Figure 4.6. For the OTO system, the ECC server and the SAP Employee Self-Service (ESS) component

are set to Relevant. SAP ESS as a Java component is created separately. This is described in the next section.

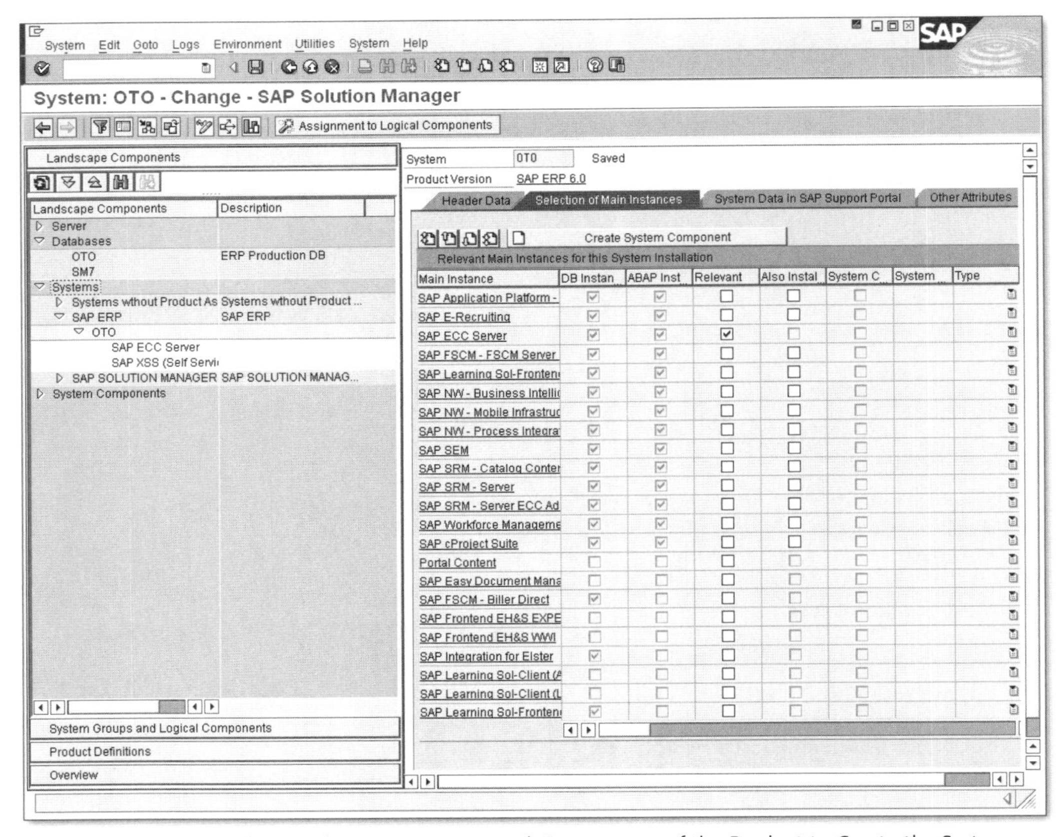

Figure 4.6 Selecting the Main Instance and Components of the Product to Create the System

7. Compile further information on the system as necessary.
8. Save your entries.

Repeat these steps for all of the systems that your solution contains.

Creating Java Components and System Components

In system components, you must manually create system components that do not correspond to ABAP technology or the status of a specific system. This provides for the links to the components. The Java component for the OTO enterprise system, the self-service, is supposed to illustrate this (see Figure 4.7).

1. Call Transaction SMSY.
2. Select the System Components landscape component.
3. In the context menu (right-clicking on the System Components landscape component), select Create New System Component.
4. Enter the necessary data. The System Component parameter refers to the system ID; for Type you're supposed to select the respective type from the input help. This example uses the Java type. For a unique identification of the component, you must also enter the installation number.
5. Save your entries.

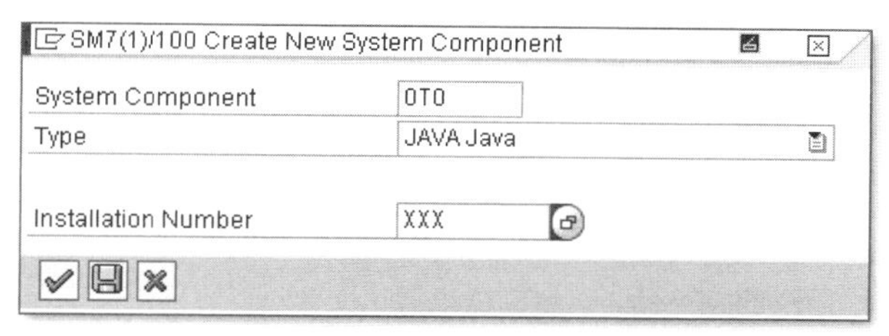

Figure 4.7 Creating the Java Component for SAP ESS

6. You can now specify information in the newly created system component. Start with maintaining the header data, and enter a message server and a database using the value selection. The manual maintenance of Java components also comprises defining the instances. For Java components, you can find this information in the system information of the component. You can call it via your browser via *http://server:HTTP PORT/sap/monitoring/SystemInfo* (see Figure 4.8).
7. Copy the Java instance information as shown in Figure 4.9 for the created Java component, and save your entries.
8. Like ABAP components, the Java component needs to be defined according to its usage. You can define the component by means of the software component. Copy the product using the Copy Software Component action. Select the Product, Product Version, and Main Instance for the component. The selection for SAP ESS is shown in Figure 4.10.

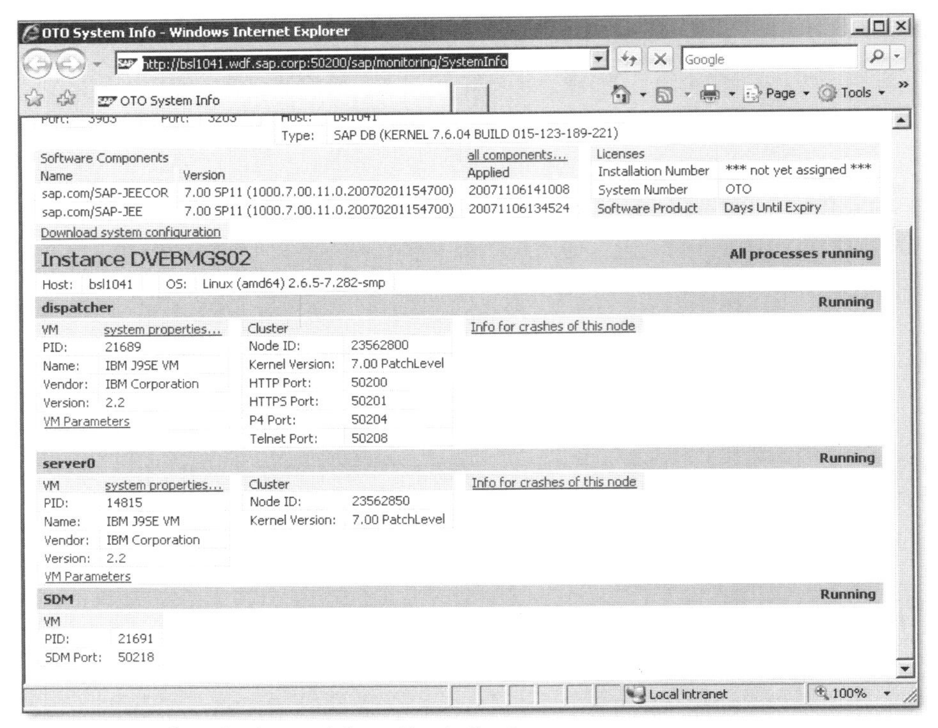

Figure 4.8 Calling the System Information in the Browser

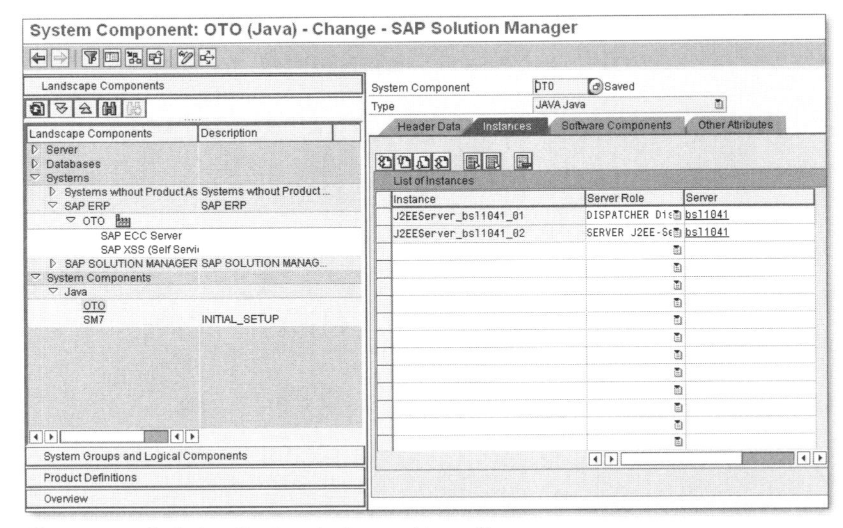

Figure 4.9 Defining the Java Instances Manually

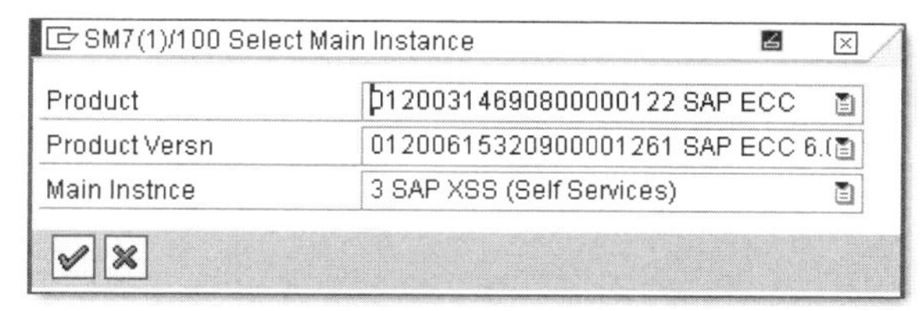

Figure 4.10 Selecting Product, Product Version, and Main Instance for the Newly Created Component

9. Save your entries.
10. To use the created component in a solution, you must link it to the main instance of the SAP system. Navigate to the selection of the main instances of the SAP system as shown in Figure 4.11, and assign the newly created system component to the main instance.
11. Save your result.

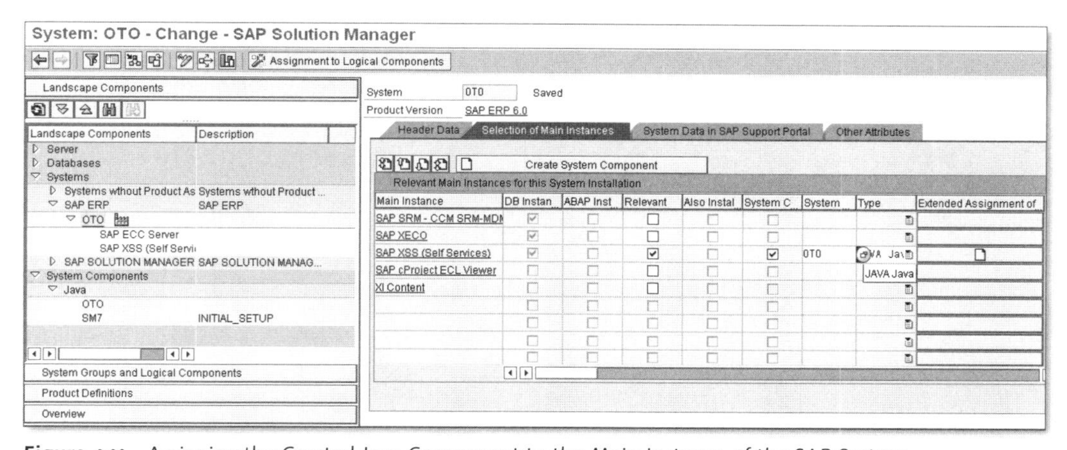

Figure 4.11 Assigning the Created Java Component to the Main Instance of the SAP System

Product Definition of Non-SAP Products

SAP Solution Manager does not recognize all non-SAP applications. Therefore, you can define non-SAP products yourself. For Toys Inc., you have to add the product WAMA.

1. Call Transaction SMSY.
2. Select the Product Definitions.

3. In the context menu (right-clicking on one of the already-existing product definitions), select Create New Product. Enter the necessary data.
4. Save your entries.
5. You can set your product as Active or Inactive. To define your system landscape you can only use active products. To define a product as Active, you must at least define one product version. The system uses this data in the system settings, where you can show and hide products. Inactive products are removed from all selection menus as a product for selection throughout SAP Solution Manager.
6. Save your entries.
7. The system displays the new product on the left-hand side of the screen, as shown in Figure 4.12.

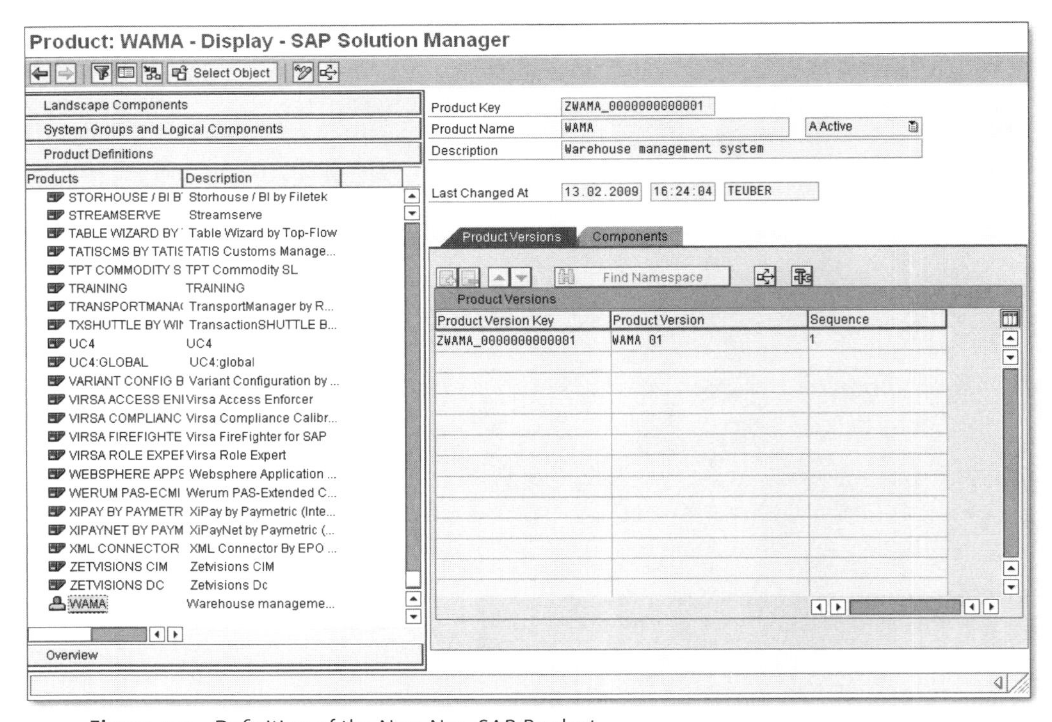

Figure 4.12 Definition of the New Non-SAP Product

4.3.2 Setting RFC Connections in Satellite Systems

Functioning RFC connections in the satellite systems are a prerequisite for monitoring system components. RFC connections can only be generated for ABAP-based main instances. Before you generate RFC connections you must meet the following requirements:

- You are authorized to log on to the destination system and to create a user there. You are authorized to create RFC connections in the local system and in the destination system.
- The satellite systems are accessible.
- The message servers are accessible on the Header Data tab in Transaction SMSY with the reference and system number supplied.

The following conditions are necessary to generate RFC connections if you use routers in your network or if the Distributed Name Service (DNS) name is required for generating an RFC connection:

- You created the message server of the satellite system in the system landscape as a host and supplied routing information for this host.
- When you created the corresponding system you specified this host as a message server.
- The system for which you want to generate RFC connections is not selected as Planned.

The following steps are necessary when generating RFC connections:

1. Call Transaction SMSY.
2. On the left-hand side of your display, select the ABAP-based main instance for which you want to generate RFC connections.
3. Switch to change mode.
4. Select a client from the Clients tab.
5. Select Generate RFC Destinations.
6. Select the type/types of RFC connections in the following dialog.
7. We recommend selecting the trusted system as the RFC connection type for SAP Solution Manager. That means you can avoid having to log on again each time you access a different component system when working with SAP Solu-

tion Manager. At the bottom of the screen, the system shows you the details of the RFC connection to be generated.

8. Specify, where necessary, a server group for load balancing in the RFC Destination Attributes section.
9. If merely providing a message server is not sufficient in your network to create an RFC connection or if you use routers in your network, take the following steps:
   - Click on the Routing Information button in the RFC Destination Attributes section.
   - The following dialog displays data about the message server. If you have not yet created the system message server as a host, this host will automatically be created and displayed on the left under Landscape Component after Transaction SMSY has been restarted.
   - Enter the IP address as necessary.
   - Enter the routing information for the Solution Manager → router → host direction.
   - Enter the routing information for the host → router → Solution Manager direction.
   - Save your entries.
10. The RFC Destinations to be Generated sections provides information on the RFC connections that are implemented when the entries have been confirmed. Check this table, and modify the entries in the upper areas, if necessary. Figure 4.13 illustrates the generation of the RFC connections for the OTO system.
11. Remote-read is preset for the system data as SAP Solution Manager needs current system data to read data on imported support packages, for example. We recommend that you do not remove the checkmark in the Actions after Generation section.
12. Select Generate RFC Destinations.
13. You will access several logon screens of the shared systems, according to the connection types selected.
14. Use the dialog user that has sufficient authorization for creating users and RFC connections to log on to the respective systems.

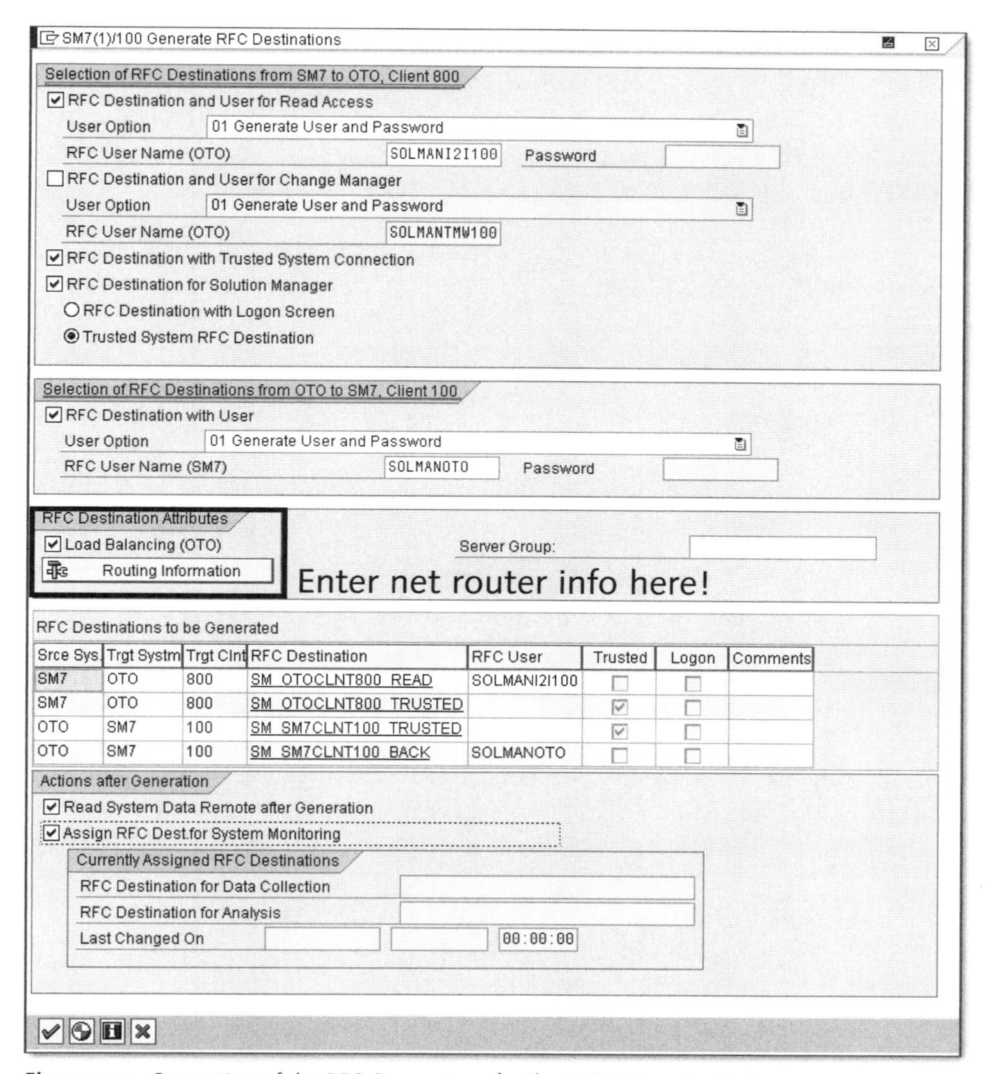

Figure 4.13 Generation of the RFC Connections for the OTO Enterprise System

If generation errors occur, proceed as follows:

1. Note details from the error message texts.
2. Troubleshoot the errors, if possible. You can enter the detail view of the RFC connection in the Configuration of RFC Destinations transaction by clicking the RFC connection in the Generate RFC Destinations dialog or by double-clicking

the RFC connection in the Clients tab. From there you can test the RFC connection and carry out any relevant changes.

3. If necessary, repeat the generation by first cancelling the old RFC connection and then regenerating it.
4. Navigate backward.

The system displays successfully generated RFC connections on the Clients tab. Repeat these steps for each system.

4.3.3 SAP Solution Data Manager

The SAP Solution Data Manager sends collected data to the SAP Service Marketplace and to the central SAP Solution Manager system. For example, weekly data can automatically be sent to SAP Solution Manager for the EarlyWatch Alert (EWA) service from all satellite systems. The SAP Solution Data Manager runs in the SAP Solution Manager system and in the satellite systems.

Currently, two versions of the SAP Solution Data Manager are available, SDCC and SDCCN. SDCCN is the version of the SAP Solution Data Manager that you should currently use, SDCC should only be used if you cannot activate SDCCN on your system.

To ensure a correct transfer of data, first check if the latest version of SDCCN is available in each system.

1. Call Transaction SDCCN. You are asked in two dialog windows if you would like to initiate a service preparation check or schedule the automatic session manager.
2. Select Service Preparation Check. You now go to RTCCTOOL. This is a tool that displays which SAP notes must be implemented for the best possible data collection. The SAP notes provide information about which add-ons — ST-A/PI or ST-PI — still need to be imported.
3. Select Automatic Session Manager (ASM) to automate collection and transfer.

The next thing you have to do is set up the Automatic Session Manager.

The ASM must be set up in the SDCCN, in all satellite systems, and in the central SAP Solution Manager system. You should use it because you need it for the EWA service.

The ASM is a periodical background job, which you can dispatch as follows:

1. Call Transaction SDCCN.
2. Follow the GoTo • Settings • Task Processor menu path. A new dialog opens.
3. Plan the execution of the background job, and set up the SAP Solution Manager server as the target system for the execution.
4. Schedule the ASM using the Activate button. You should start the job during a period of low system load.
5. Save your entries.

To send monitoring data to SAP Solution Manager and to SAP, check if the RFC connections for the data transfer are correctly defined:

1. Call Transaction SMSY.
2. Follow the Environment • Solution Manager Operations • Administration SDCCN menu path. A new dialog opens.
3. Add all of the systems via the Add Systems button. When you confirm this selection, the system immediately checks if the connection to the system is defined and fully functional. The system checks the connection of the satellite system for possible connections of the SAP Solution Data Manager to SAP or other SAP Solution Managers and lists the result in a table.
4. For all systems, activate SDCCN, and check to see if the *master* role is assigned to the SAP Solution Manager system. If the master role has not been assigned yet, assign it to the system using the Master System button.
5. Save your entries.

An RFC connection to SAP Solution Manager is necessary to send data from the satellite system to SAP Solution Manager. To do this, the connection that was already created in Section 4.3.2, Setting RFC Connections in Satellite Systems, was used here. The *back connection* primarily serves to transfer data for the EWA and the service level report.

4.4 Solution Landscapes in SAP Solution Manager

The first step in setting up system monitoring in SAP Solution Manager is creating an active solution. This section describes the creation of a solution landscape in SAP Solution Manager 7.0.

4.4.1 Overview of Active Solutions

In the SAP Solution Manager environment a solution landscape is also abbreviated to "solution." In the entry screen in Transaction Solution_Manager you can gain an overview of all of the active solutions. There is a status overview for every solution. The example in Figure 4.14 gives you a status overview of all active solutions.

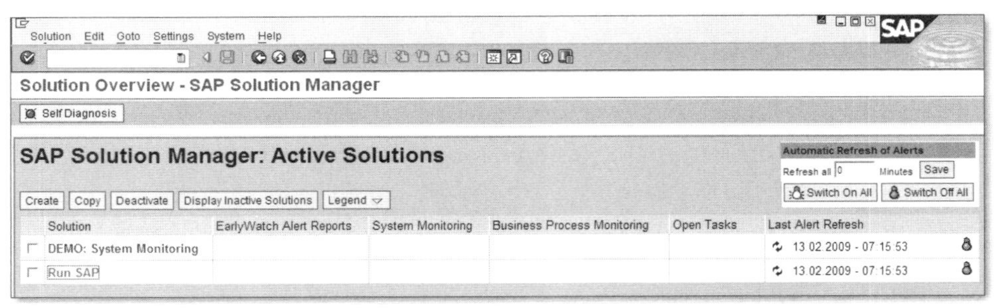

Figure 4.14 Solution Overview in SAP Solution Manager

The SAP Solution Manager overview provides a status overview for every solution of the following areas:

- **EWA Reports**
  This area gives you an overview of the rating of all systems of the EWA Report solution. The last generation status of all reports is used as the basis here.
- **System Monitoring**
  Here you gain a complete overview of the monitoring of your system components. From this description you can see the number of objects for which an alarm exists (red or yellow), and the number of objects that don't contain any problems (green). From here you can get a direct graphic overview of the system monitoring of the solution.
- **Business Process Monitoring**
  As is the case in Components/System you get preliminary status information about business process monitoring with regard to the number of objects for which an alarm was triggered.

  The status shows the number of objects (projects, processes, or services) in red, yellow, or green. Red traffic lights indicate serious errors have been detected or alerts with a high severity level have been issued. This means that the system operation is endangered. Yellow traffic lights advise of problems that you should be aware of but are not completely critical at this time. That means that the OS is not under threat. Green traffic lights indicate that a monitored value is in a permitted area.

- **Open Tasks**
  This area provides a status for the manual system administration. It displays both successful completions and open activities. You can view the total number of alerts for all activities of the solution.

4.4.2 Creating the "System Monitoring" Solution

Whether you want to combine all of your satellite systems in one solution landscape or distribute them over several solutions is a matter of preference. You can group solutions by various requirements or aspects. There are some recommendations, which you should include in your considerations, but the implementation itself is up to you. However, you shouldn't group by production systems, test systems, and development systems. The solution landscapes should be grouped by organizational aspects. For example, you could use regions or areas that are used in SAP Solution Manager for grouping.

1. Call Transaction Solution_Manager, and navigate to the solution overview. An overview of the active solutions is displayed.
2. Click on the Create button. A new dialog opens (see Figure 4.15).

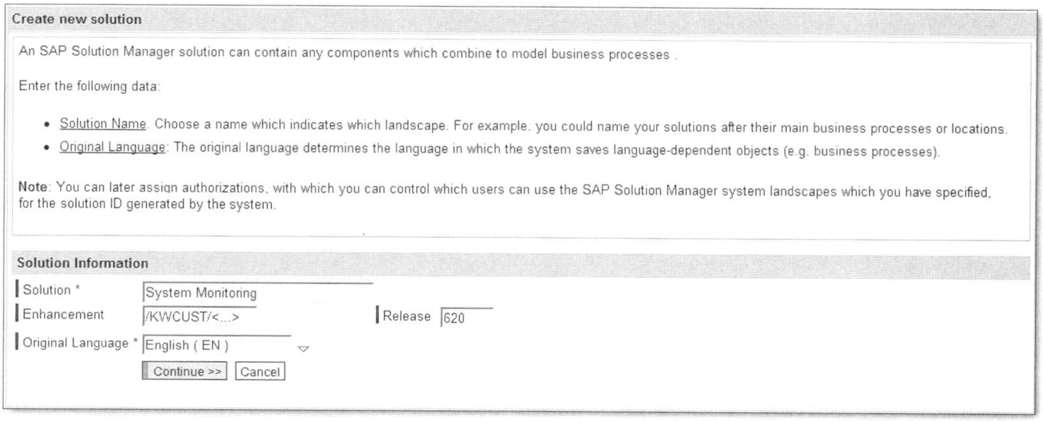

Create new solution

An SAP Solution Manager solution can contain any components which combine to model business processes .

Enter the following data:

- Solution Name. Choose a name which indicates which landscape. For example, you could name your solutions after their main business processes or locations.
- Original Language: The original language determines the language in which the system saves language-dependent objects (e.g. business processes).

Note: You can later assign authorizations, with which you can control which users can use the SAP Solution Manager system landscapes which you have specified, for the solution ID generated by the system.

Solution Information

Solution * System Monitoring
Enhancement /KWCUST/<...> Release 620
Original Language * English (EN)
Continue >> Cancel

Figure 4.15 Dialog for Creating a New Solution

3. Enter a name for the solution landscape in the Solution field. Select a name for the solution landscape that signifies which landscape it belongs to. In our example it is called System Monitoring.
4. Define the solution language. All language-dependent objects (for example, business processes) are stored in this language.
5. Save the settings by clicking the Continue button.
6. The new solution is created and the Solution Landscape screen is displayed. The newly created solution is empty at first. You must now assign the systems to be monitored and managed to the solution. For example, for subsequent authorization assignments, an ID is assigned to the solution, which is displayed in the lower part of the first screen.

4.4.3 Deactivating an Active Solution

You can deactivate solution landscapes that are no longer used. You cannot display any services in a deactivated solution and you cannot make any changes.

1. Call Transaction Solution_Manager.
2. Select the solution landscape by setting a flag in the empty checkbox on the left of the solution description.
3. Click on the Deactivate button.
4. If you would like to view all deactivated solution landscapes, then click on the Display Inactive solutions button. You will see all deactivated solutions in a new dialog. You can reactivate deactivated solutions at any time by clicking on the Activate button.

4.5 Configuration of the "System Monitoring" Solution

In the next step, the *System Monitoring* solution is assigned to the systems included in the system monitoring. But first, let's look at the structure of the main SAP Solution Manager screen.

4.5.1 The Basic Structure of the Main Screen of a Solution Landscape

The main screen of an active solution in SAP Solution Manager consists of a work area with the navigation bar in the upper part of the window and a separate navigation area in the left part of the window so that you can navigate between the three main sections. The screen is divided into the Solution Landscape, Operations Setup and Operations sections. Figure 4.16 displays the main screen.

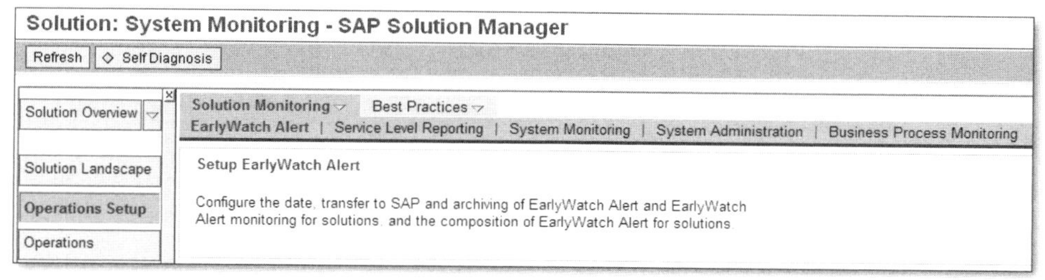

Figure 4.16 Work Area of SAP Solution Manager

- **Operations Setup**
  The Operations Setup area enables you to set and configure SAP Solution Manager tools, which you use to operate your system landscape. Various service categories are provided, which can then be structured into different subsections. These subsections may have a work area.

  Table 4.5 gives you an overview and an explanation of the individual service categories and their subsections:

Service Category	Subsections/Function
Solution monitoring	Setup ▸ of EWAs ▸ of service level reports ▸ of system monitoring ▸ of system administration ▸ of business process monitoring
Best Practices	Success methods for the following areas: ▸ Change Request Management (ChaRM) ▸ Configuration Management ▸ Availability Management ▸ Capacity Management ▸ Service Level Management ▸ Funding Management

Table 4.5 Categories in Operations Setup of SAP Solution Manager 7.0

- **Operations**
  By selecting Operations you use the functionalities that you already set up in the Operations Setup area. The Operations area is divided into the areas and subcategories listed in Table 4.6.

Service Category	Function
Solution monitoring	▶ EWA ▶ Service level reporting ▶ System monitoring/administration ▶ Business process monitoring
Service Desk	Integrating message processing for your own support organization with the option to forward messages to SAP Support
Change Management	Using the functions of Software Change Management. The MOPZ is a component of this service (integral part as of April 2007) to maintain support packages for NetWeaver 2004s systems
Solution reporting	Option for solution-wide evaluations in a report via the SAP Solution Manager services
Service plan	▶ Using SAP services ▶ Access control to SAP Service Marketplace ▶ Overview of certifications
Issue Management	Managing your issues

Table 4.6 Categories in the Operations Area of SAP Solution Manager 7.0

4.5.2 Integrating the Systems in System Monitoring

After creating the solution landscape you should assign the systems to it. This means the only systems integrated into system monitoring are those already created in Transaction SMSY. You can also incorporate additional systems into the solution landscape at a later stage.

To include individual systems in a landscape, you must first assign them to a logical component. This ensures that all systems in a system line (production, quality assurance, development system) are assigned to one object. This is to ensure the transparency of the system landscape and optimize the maintenance effort for a landscape modification.

To create a logical component, proceed as follows:

1. Use the left navigation bar to go to the solution landscape.
2. Select the system landscape maintenance. This returns you to Transaction SMSY.
3. Within the navigation, select System Groups and Logical Components and expand the Logical Components tree.
4. Instead of creating the logical components for a system, you should create them for a product. You then add all involved systems to this component. Navigate to the product version you want to create the logical component for, open the context menu, and select Create New Logical Component.
5. Enter a meaningful name for the logical component in the customer namespace to clearly identify it. Select the appropriate product and version for the systems you created in Transaction SMSY.
6. Confirm and save your entries with OK.
7. The system displays the new logical component in the left part of the screen. Assign the systems to the logical component using the value selection.
8. Save your entries, and repeat the steps for all of your system lines.

Figure 4.17 illustrates the system assignment.

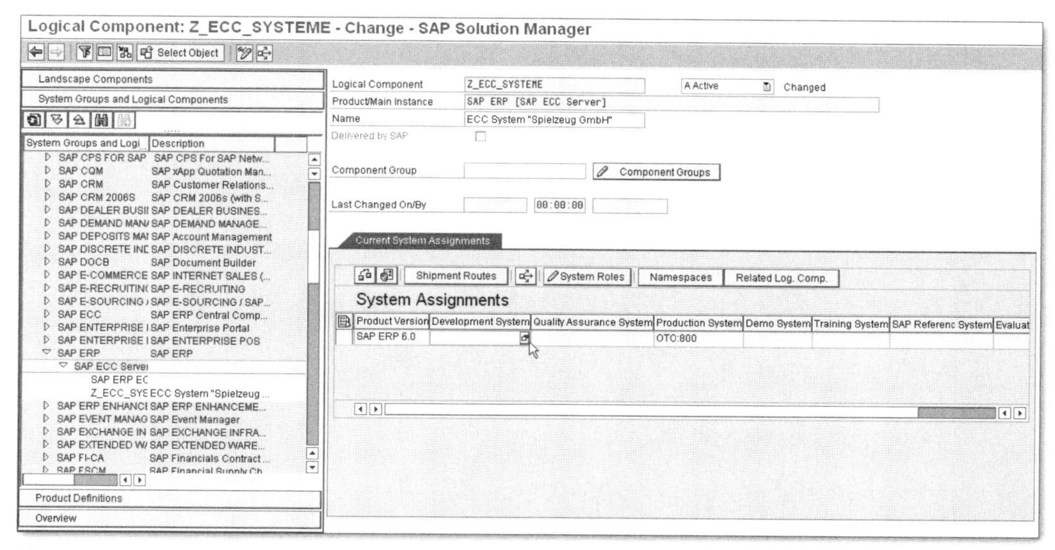

Figure 4.17 System Assignment in a Logical Component Using the Enterprise Systems of Toys Inc. as an Example

In the Toys Inc. example, all systems are first assigned to the active solution, System Monitoring. The actual relevance of the individual systems is defined during the configuration of the landscape.

1. In the SAP Solution Manager navigation bar select Solution Landscape.
2. Select Solution Landscape Management. A new dialog opens.
3. Select the logical components for your solution using the value selection.
4. You can activate or deactivate the systems for the solution landscapes separately in the overview. All systems that are highlighted in green are active for the solution and can be used for the scenarios in SAP Solution Manager. Gray systems are not relevant for the scenarios and are not included (see Figure 4.18).
5. Save your settings, and return to the work area of SAP Solution Manager.

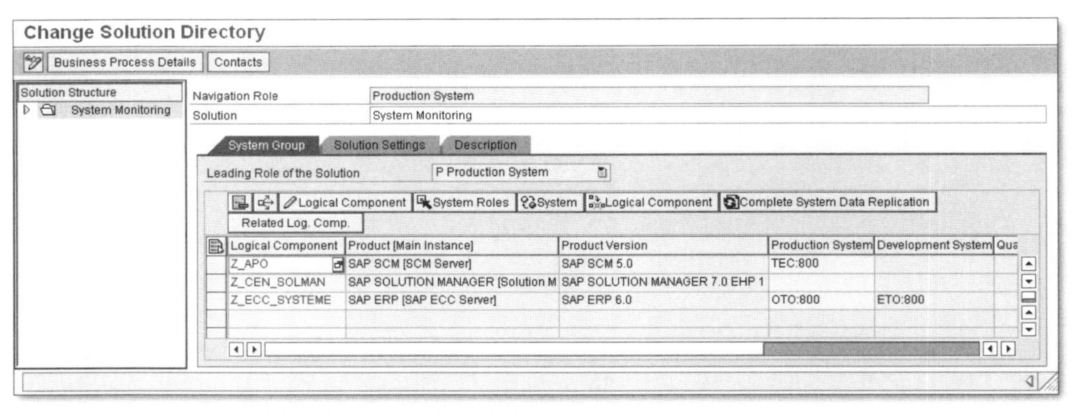

Figure 4.18 Adding Systems to the Solution

The systems are displayed in SAP Solution Manager for operation. The newly added systems now appear in the solution graphic for SAP systems.

4.5.3 Assigning RFC Connections for System Monitoring

For security reasons, two RFC connections are created to monitor the satellite systems, because there are two main differences in the requirements for the monitoring and monitored systems.

- **RFC destination for data collection**
  Data collection methods are active in the monitored system, which stores monitor attributes in shared memory. The monitoring system reads these values through

an RFC call with a specific user name. In the system being monitored, this user is merely an observer who has to log on for each query. For this destination you should use the user of the RFC generation (SOLMAN<SID>CLNT<client>), which can only call certain function modules.

- **RFC destination for analysis**
  If a data collection method raises an alarm, you can start an analysis method in the monitoring monitor for the monitoring attribute. You can make changes in the system being monitored, which require further authorization. Use a dialog user for this.

You can assign RFC connections for the centralized system monitoring in the operation mode of your solution landscape in SAP Solution Manager:

1. Select Solution Landscape.
2. Select System Landscape Maintenance. This returns you to Transaction SMSY.
3. Follow the menu path: LANDSCAPE COMPONENT • SYSTEMS • <APPLICATION COMPONENT> • <SYSTEM>.
4. Select the corresponding hardware component. You will find information on the hardware on the right-hand side of the screen.
5. Select the Clients tab, as shown in Figure 4.19.

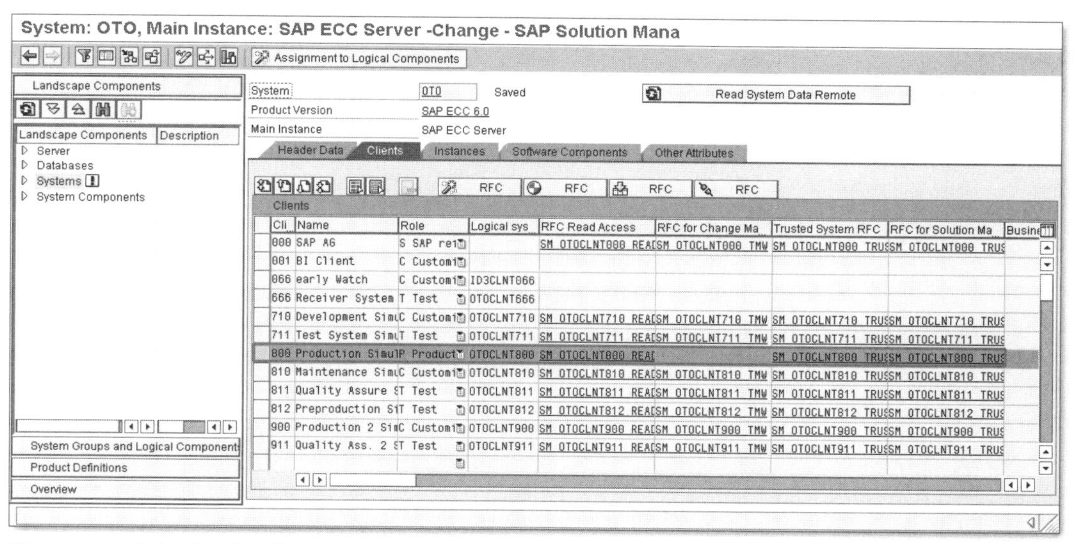

Figure 4.19 Selecting the Client to Be Monitored Using the OTO Enterprise System Example

6. Select the row of the client to assign RFC connections to.
7. Click on the Assign and Check RFC Destinations button. A new dialog opens.
8. Select the Assign RFC Destination For System Monitoring field, as shown in Figure 4.20. You only need to use this option for one client per system.
9. Save your entries.

The required RFC destinations are assigned to a system. You can find an overview of the monitored remote systems in Transaction RZ21 via the TECHNICAL INFRASTRUCTURE • DISPLAY TOPOLOGY menu path on the Monitored, Remote SAP Systems tab.

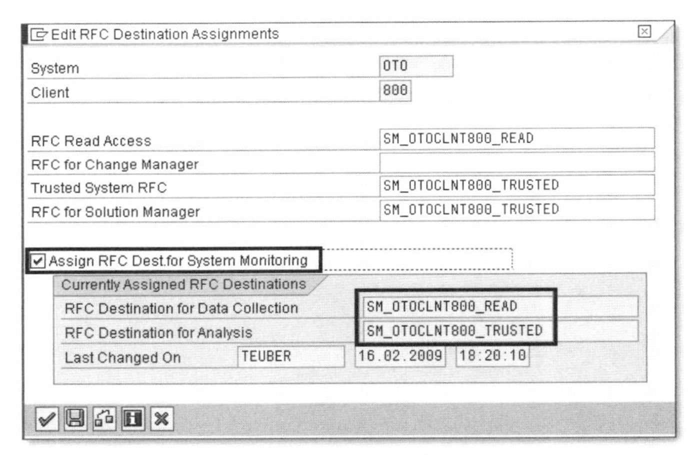

Figure 4.20 Assigning RFC Destinations for System Monitoring

4.5.4 CCMS Agents in Central Monitoring

To enable central system monitoring, you need the agent technology for the CCMS. This technology forms the basis for transfers and also avoids unwanted monitoring inconsistencies. Central system monitoring is characterized by the fact that you can use SAP Solution Manager to implement settings and track or analyze terminations of systems that are supposed to be monitored. If an agent is registered for a satellite system, the agent automatically loses the right to own the shared memory in which the objects and their descriptions are stored.

As a result, the central monitoring system overwrites manual changes to an object, for example, the modification of the threshold values in a satellite system. The system can no longer make decisions for objects that are also managed (or monitored) by the central monitoring system.

You can register CCMS agents during live operations of the satellite and monitoring system:

1. Download the latest version of the CCMS agents from the SAP Service Marketplace. You can find the agents in a package of the database-independent kernel of the satellite system.
2. Extract the agent package and copy the agents to the satellite system under */usr/sap/ccms*.
3. Log on as <SID>adm at the OS level of the satellite system and start a console.
4. Start the agent registration as described in the documentation.

Example for Starting the Registration for the OTO System for Linux:

```
sapccm4x -R pf=/usr/sap/OTO/SYS/profile/OTO_DVEBMSG02_bs11041
```

5. Transfer the required parameters to the configuration file. The agent registration only queries user information of the central monitoring system but not of the monitored system. The agent doesn't have to communicate with the monitored system; it merely uses the status information of the shared memory.
6. You can check for the successful registration in SAP Solution Manager. Call Transaction RZ21 and start the topology overview. The Agents for the CEN System tab should display the new agent and its connection.

For a more detailed description and additional notes that describe the handling of agents, refer to the CCMS agents guide in the SAP Service Marketplace.

4.5.5 EWA

The EWA is a monitoring tool that monitors the administrative areas of SAP components and provides you with updates on the performance and stability of the solution landscape. The EWA runs automatically once a week. You can generate a report for each EWA run. The report contains information on the system status, performance, system configuration, system operation, system administration, and so on.

The following sections explain how you can generate and view the EWA report:

1. Select Operations on the left side of the screen.
2. Follow the Solution Monitoring • EarlyWatch Alert menu path. You will get an overview of the EWA services for all SAP systems. From here you can generate the report as an HTML document or as an MS Word document.
   - HTML document
     1. Select a link to an EWA service.
     2. Select the report type. The report is generated.
   - Word document
     1. Select the Generate Word Report symbol in the Activities column.
     2. Select the report type. The report is generated.
     3. Save the generated report if you want to view it at a later stage.

4.6 Setting up Active System Monitoring

In this section we will implement the system monitoring requirements and learn how to set up system monitoring. The monitoring concept created for Toys Inc. in Chapter 3, Designing the Monitoring Concepts, will form the basis for the setup. Please note that the setup and maintenance of monitoring objects in SAP Solution Manager 7.0 is described using monitoring objects that are contained in the active monitoring process. Furthermore, a complete description of the implementation of the monitoring concept doesn't need to be repeated for each of the three systems, as the configuration steps are the same each time. The following section also discusses how the setup procedure affects other systems. You should carry out the following steps in the order described.

4.6.1 Basic Principles on the Structure of the "Setup System Monitoring" Service

Let's first take a look at the structure of the screen for the *Setup System Monitoring* service. You must be in the active solution in which you want to set up system monitoring. Take the following steps to get there:

1. Select Operations Setup.
2. Follow the menu path Solution Monitoring • System Monitoring • Setup System Monitoring. You are now in the system monitoring configuration service, as illustrated in Figure 4.21.

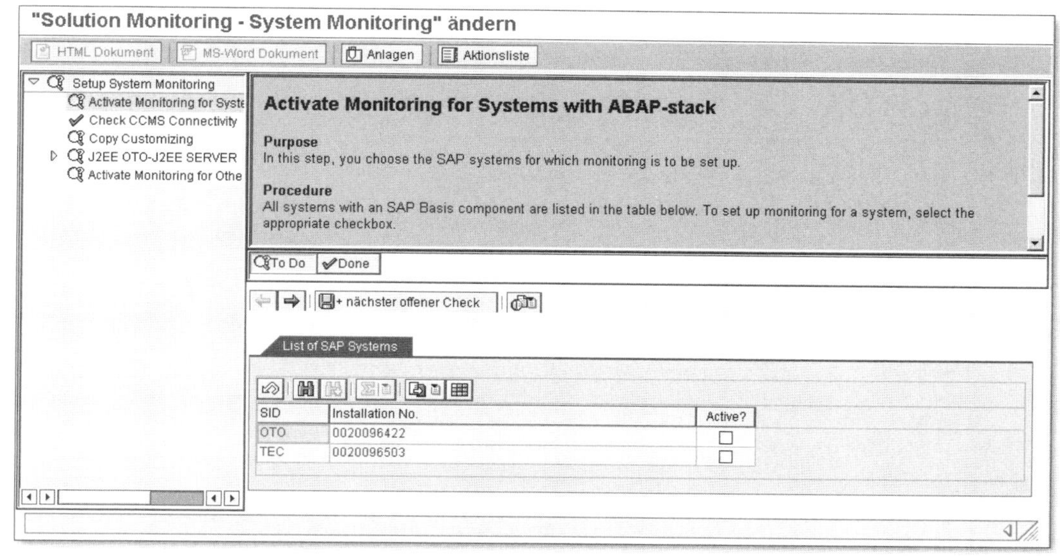

Figure 4.21 Initial Screen for the System Monitoring Setup

The screen is divided into three functional areas. In the left pane of the dialog is a tree structure with the checks you need to set up system monitoring. The following checks are available:

- General checks
  - Monitoring activation
  - Setup of RFC connections for monitoring
  - Copy Customizing
- System-specific subchecks
  - Monitoring setup for SAP systems
  - User-defined alerts
- Additional components (optional)
  - Additional software components (Java, liveCache, Text Retrieval and Extraction (TREX))

The upper right-hand pane of the system monitoring configuration dialog provides an action-specific description and background information on whichever check you are in.

In the bottom left-hand pane you can see the tables that you maintain for each check. This is where you can enter threshold value definitions for the monitoring objects, for example.

4.6.2 Activating System Monitoring for SAP Systems with an ABAP Kernel

Upon activation, you receive predefined standard monitoring objects that you can use as a basis for the active system monitoring setup. To activate system monitoring, proceed as follows for the setup:

1. You are in your solution landscape in the Setup System Monitoring service.
2. Select Activate Monitoring on the left-hand side of the screen. To the right of the screen is a list of SAP systems, which in this solution landscape you can include in system monitoring as shown in Figure 4.22.

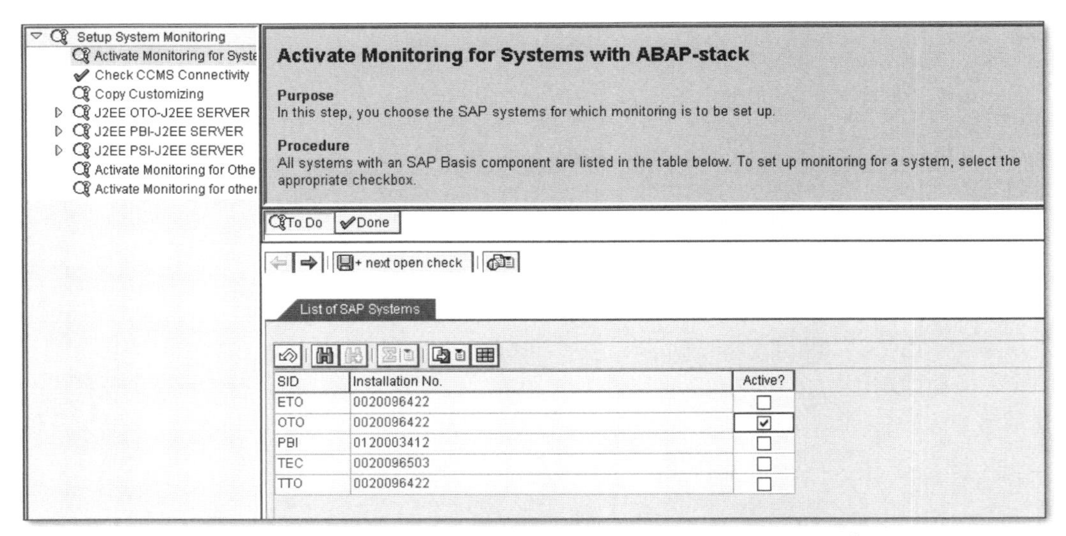

Figure 4.22 System Monitoring Service — Activating the System Monitoring for Systems of the Landscape

3. In the Active column, check the systems to be included in monitoring.
4. Save your entries. For every activated system, the system adds an additional node in the left tree structure. You will recognize the check from the sequence of characters: SAP System <SID> <Installation Number>.

4.6.3 RFC Connections for System Monitoring

Two RFC connections are necessary for system monitoring, one for data collection and one for analysis. Section 4.5.3, Assigning RFC Connections for System Monitoring, already described how you can assign RFC connections. If this step is performed, then a green rating automatically appears in the Status column, as you can see in Figure 4.23. In this figure, the connections for data collection and analysis for the OTO, PBI, and TEC production systems of Toys Inc. have been successfully created.

The rating only indicates whether RFC connections have been assigned to the data collection and analysis. If the system displays a red rating, the RFC connections may have been created but they weren't assigned to system monitoring. In this case, proceed as described in Section 4.5.3, Assigning RFC Connections for System Monitoring. In addition, you should check the functioning of the RFC connections. This is not automatically done in the status message.

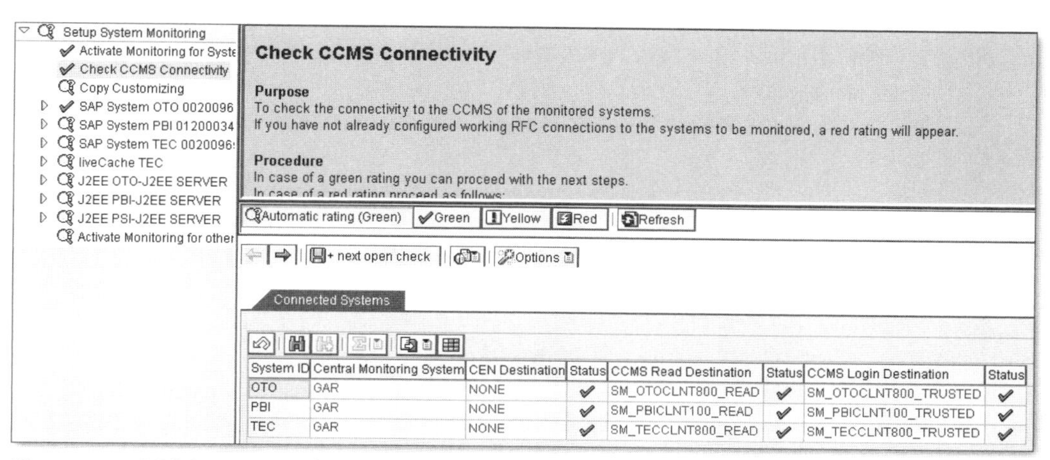

Figure 4.23 RFC Connections for System Monitoring

4.6.4 Setting Up System Monitoring for SAP Components

System monitoring for SAP components is set up under the system-specific subchecks. These subchecks refer to the individual SAP systems contained in the solution landscape for which the system monitoring was activated. According to your requirements, you can use predefined standard monitoring objects or individual user-defined objects. Please note that the monitoring objects in the CCMS must be accessible, because the CCMS provides the information for the agents and the RFC connections.

The Toys Inc. example explains where some alerts can be integrated.

First, we have to set up the monitoring of the OS. According to the Toys Inc. monitoring concept, the file systems, CPUs, memory consumption, OS collector, and swap space are monitored. The following steps show you how to activate the monitoring objects for the OS:

1. Begin in the Setup System Monitoring service.
2. Follow the SYSTEM MONITORING CUSTOMIZING • SAP SYSTEM <SID> <INSTALLATION NUMBER> • SERVER <HOST NAME> • SETUP MONITORING FOR SERVER <HOST NAME> menu path. Maintain the standard monitoring objects CPU, paging, OS collector, and file system and their threshold values.
3. Save your entries.
4. Follow the SYSTEM MONITORING CUSTOMIZING • SAP SYSTEM <SID> <INSTALLATION NUMBER> • SERVER <HOST NAME> • USER DEFINED ALERTS FOR <HOST NAME> menu path to set up the swap space for monitoring.
5. Select the monitoring object in the selection field in the Alert Name column and click the Transfer button.
6. Save your entries.

Next, you must set up instance availability and system availability monitoring.

The prerequisite for checking the instance and system availability is the installation of the CCMSPING agent. You can install and configure this agent on any host. Using the agent means the availability of systems can be controlled centrally. Section 4.5.4, CCMS Agents in Central Monitoring, provides more information on the installation of CCMS agents.

When the agent is being used, carry out the following activities to set up instance-availability monitoring in SAP Solution Manager:

1. Begin in the Setup System Monitoring service.
2. Follow the System Monitoring Customizing • SAP System <SID> <Installation Number> • SAP Application Server <Instance> • Instance Availability of <Instance> menu path.
3. Activate the Instance Status alert.
4. Save your entries.

System availability should be superordinate to all instances. It is therefore advisable to activate system availability via the menu path: System Monitoring Customizing • SAP System <SID> <Installation Number> • User Defined Alerts <SID> <Installation Number>.

The next step is setting up system performance monitoring. There is a range of standard monitoring objects available for system performance.

1. Begin in the Setup System Monitoring service.
2. Follow the System Monitoring Customizing • SAP System <SID> <Installation Number> • SAP Application Server <Instance> • Performance Alerts of <Instance> menu path. Activate the monitoring objects according to the specifications of your monitoring concept.
3. Save your entries.
4. If the monitoring objects are not set as standard in SAP Solution Manager, then follow the System Monitoring Customizing • SAP- System <SID> <Installation Number> • SAP Application Server <Instance> • User Defined Alerts of <Instance> menu path to check. At this point enter the missing monitoring objects.
5. Save your entries.

After that, database monitoring must be set up. You can set criteria to monitor database performance and administrative monitoring objects as follows:

1. Begin in the Setup System Monitoring service.
2. Follow the System Monitoring Customizing • SAP System <SID> <Installation Number> • Database <SID>-DATABASE menu path. Activate the monitoring objects in the underlying checks according to the specifications of your monitoring concept.
3. Save your entries.

4. If the monitoring concept does not set monitoring objects as standard in SAP Solution Manager, follow the SYSTEM MONITORING CUSTOMIZING • SAP SYSTEM <SID> <INSTALLATION NUMBER> • DATABASE <SID>-DATABASE • USER DEFINED ALERTS FOR <SID>-DATABASE menu path to check. Enter the missing alerts at this point.
5. Save your entries.

4.6.5 Copying System Monitoring Configuration Settings

The system monitoring settings that you have set for an SAP component can be transferred to other SAP components, too. To do this, copy the monitoring object settings. You can implement this for the database instance, the ABAP system, the server, and the database. Please note that the database copy mechanism only functions with similar database types.

1. Begin in the Setup System Monitoring service.
2. Follow the menu path SYSTEM MONITORING CUSTOMIZING • COPY CUSTOMIZING.
3. Select from the context if you want to copy the alert settings to the instance, the ABAP system, the server, or the database.
4. Select the source and target systems.
5. Click on the Copy button and save the entries to trigger the copying mechanism. The settings conform to the corresponding target component.

4.6.6 Setting Up System Monitoring for Additional SAP Components — liveCache

Toys Inc. uses the SAP Advanced Planner and Optimizer (APO) solution in their enterprise. Configuration steps for general system monitoring of SAP components have already been described earlier in this book. This section shows you how to set up the monitoring for the liveCache, another component in SAP APO.

Proceed as follows:

1. Begin in the Setup System Monitoring service.
2. Follow the SYSTEM MONITORING CUSTOMIZING • LIVECACHE <SID>-LIVECACHE menu path.
3. Select the APO system in which the liveCache is active and the related CCMS context using the F4 help.

4. Save your entries.
5. Follow the SYSTEM MONITORING CUSTOMIZING • LIVECACHE <SID> LIVECACHE • ERRORS/ADMINISTRATING OF <SID>-LIVECACHE menu path. Activate the corresponding monitoring objects according to the monitoring concept.
6. Save your entries.
7. Follow the SYSTEM MONITORING CUSTOMIZING • LIVECACHE <SID>-LIVECACHE • PERFORMANCE/AVAILABILITY OF <SID>-LIVECACHE menu path. Activate the corresponding monitoring objects according to the monitoring concept.
8. Save your entries.
9. If the monitoring concept does not set certain monitoring objects as standard in SAP Solution Manager, follow the SYSTEM MONITORING CUSTOMIZING • MONITORING CUSTOMIZING • LIVECACHE <SID>-LIVECACHE • USER DEFINED ALERTS FOR <SID>-LIVECACHE menu path to check. At this point enter the missing objects.
10. Save your entries.

4.6.7 Setting Up System Monitoring for Java 2 Enterprise Edition (J2EE) SAP Components

Toys Inc. uses different solutions in their enterprise that are partly based on SAP NetWeaver Application Server (AS) Java technologies. Configuration steps for general system monitoring of SAP components have already been described earlier in this book. This section shows you how to set up monitoring for additional Java components as components of SAP products.

Proceed as follows:

1. Begin in the Setup System Monitoring service.
2. Follow the SYSTEM MONITORING CUSTOMIZING • J2EE <SID>-J2EE SERVER menu path.
3. Select the central monitoring system. This property is generated with the CCMS agents on the satellite systems. The SAPCCMSR agent is a prerequisite for the J2EE component of the satellite system.
4. Because the monitoring concept does not set the monitoring objects as standard in SAP Solution Manager, follow the SYSTEM MONITORING CUSTOMIZING • J2EE <SID>-J2EE SERVER • USER DEFINED ALERTS FOR J2EE <SID>-J2EE SERVER menu path to check. At this point enter the missing objects.
5. Save your entries.

4.6.8 Setting up System Monitoring for Additional Hardware Components

In addition to SAP system hardware, the hardware of non-SAP systems can also be monitored. The CCMS monitoring objects just need to be recognized in the central monitoring system. This means that data about OS resources of non-SAP components can be collected if, as described in Chapter 3, Designing the Monitoring Concepts, the SAPCCMSR and SAPOSCOL agents are installed.

In the Toys Inc. example, the non-SAP application, WAMA, runs on its own host. This host's OS data should be monitored according to the monitoring concept.

1. Begin in the Setup System Monitoring service.
2. Follow the System Monitoring Customizing • Additional Hardware Components menu path.
3. For the Type column select NON-SAP-APPLICATION, and in the Name column specify the system ID of the system to be monitored.
4. Save your entries. Depending on the selection, further checks may be carried out for the relevant server.
5. Follow the System Monitoring Customizing • Additional Hardware Components • Hardware Component Server <host name> menu path. Select the CCMS context for the server.
6. Save your entries.
7. Follow the System Monitoring Customizing • Additional Hardware Components • Alert Customizing of NON-SAP-APPLICATION <SID> menu path. Activate the corresponding monitoring objects according to the monitoring concept.
8. Save your entries.
9. If the monitoring concept does not set certain monitoring objects as standard in SAP Solution Manager, follow the System Monitoring Customizing • Monitoring Customizing • Additional Hardware Components • Alert Customizing of NON-SAP-APPLICATION <SID> menu path to check. At this point, enter the missing objects.
10. Save your entries.

4.7 The SAP Solution Manager Alert Monitor

Alerts are a central element in monitoring IT landscapes because they provide fast and reliable reports or warnings. These alerts are displayed in the Alert Monitor.

4.7.1 Basic Principles of the Alert Monitor

Before we provide a graphical overview of the system components and their monitoring objects and alerts in SAP Solution Manager, let's discuss some general information on the Alert Monitor. The Alert Monitor concept comes from the CCMS world and can also be transferred to SAP Solution Manager. You can view alerts from the various monitoring objects in both CCMS (via Transaction RZ20) and in SAP Solution Manager. However, the display of both areas is entirely different. From a functional perspective, there is no difference, because SAP Solution Manager reverts to the monitoring architecture of the CCMS.

There are two different views in the Alert Monitor.

- **Current Status**
  The Current status view gives information on the latest reported data on the components. The color of the individual monitoring objects (red, yellow, or green) shows their status at that time and is independent of open alerts. The threshold value of a monitoring object can be been exceeded or under-run. The result is a yellow or red alert in the current overview display. During the next data collection, the value is once again in the green area. The result is that the current status of the monitoring object changes back to green.

  Figure 4.24 shows currently open alerts for Instance bsl1041_OTO_02 at Toys Inc. in SAP Solution Manager. For the Aborted jobs monitoring object, for example, the system displays a red alert. To analyze this alert, simply click on the alert description to navigate to the system that is monitored. The [More] link provides a description of the object, which enables you to analyze the error in the proper context at any time.

- **Open Alerts**
  Open alerts show all problems that have not yet been analyzed by the system administrator. Additional details regarding some of the alerts are shown in the Alert Monitor. These details contain information on the current threshold value and the current value that has exceeded or fallen short of the threshold value

and caused the alarm. You can get information on other alerts if you go directly to the monitored system.

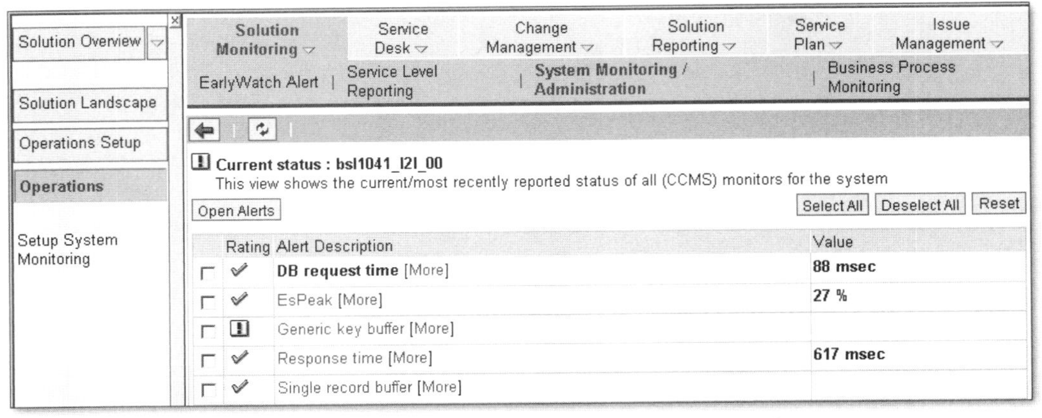

Figure 4.24 Alert Monitor in SAP Solution Manager — View: Current Status

4.7.2 The Alert Monitor after the Setup Process for System Monitoring

After completing the setup for the monitoring objects and defining threshold values for each alert, you can see the result immediately after the next data collection in the graphic overview:

1. Begin in the active solution.
2. Follow the Operations System • Monitoring/Administration menu path.
3. You are now in the system group overview. In Figure 4.25 you can see system components based on our example of system monitoring for Toys Inc.

Each system component contains at least one subcomponent. To view details on the system components, select the respective components. The specified monitoring objects for the components with their values at that time appear.

Figure 4.26 shows the operating system alerts for the OTO system with the bsl1041 host. To the right of the alerts you can view the values. On the left-hand side, in the Rating column, the current status of the last reported data is highlighted in color.

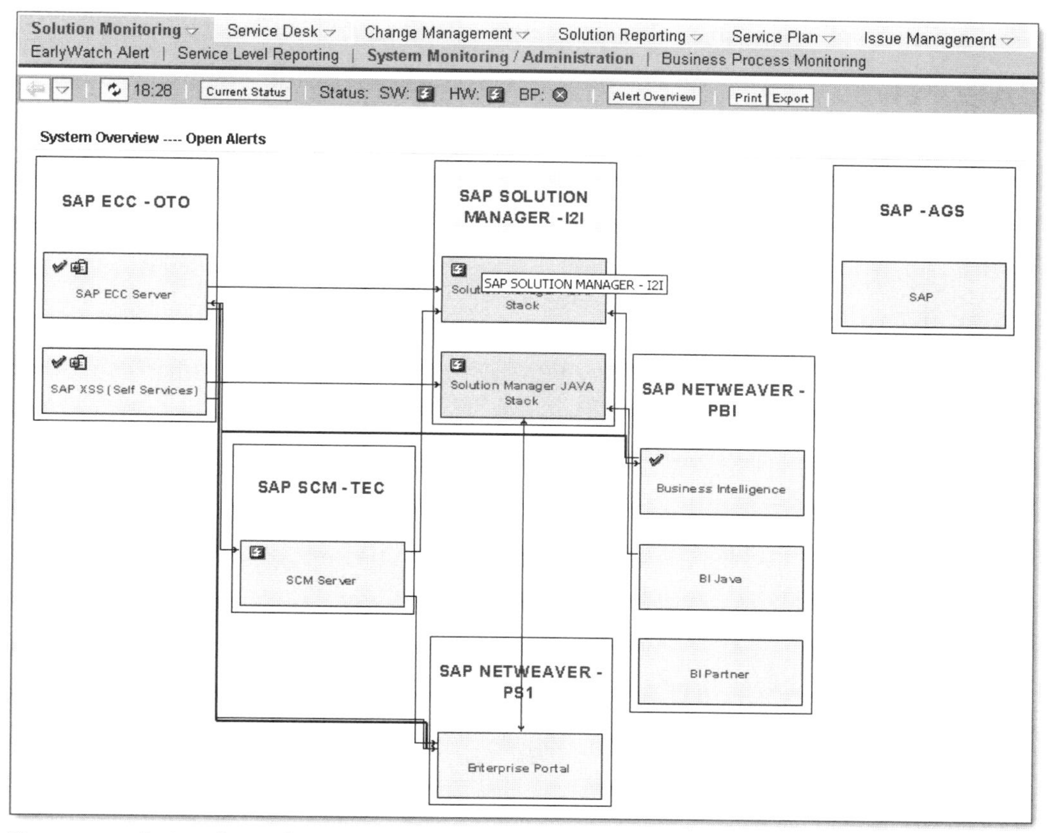

Figure 4.25 System Group Overview

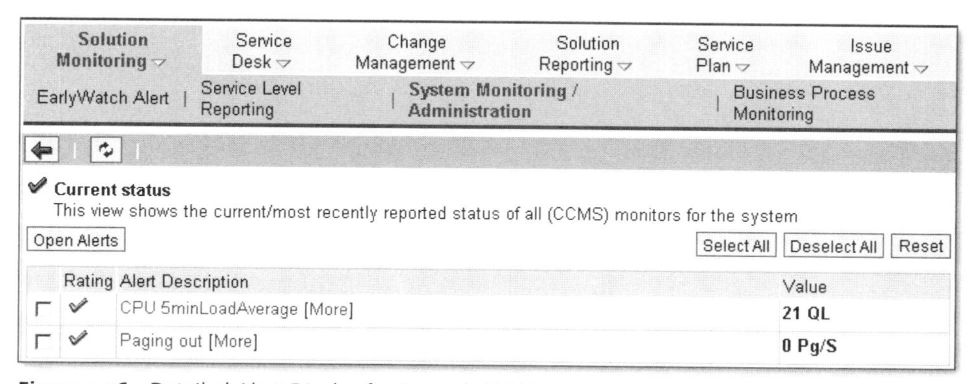

Figure 4.26 Detailed Alert Display for Server bsl1041

4.8 Performance Monitoring in AS Java Environments

To monitor AS Java systems, you can use CA Wily Technology products. The End-to-End Root Cause Analysis tools enable you to obtain performance information for any system across the entire landscape in accordance with the product to which the system belongs. The following does not describe the implementation of the End-to-End Root Cause Analysis tools but how you can use the tools to gain a detailed overview of your solution.

1. Call Solution Manager Diagnostics in your browser and log on to the system using the SAPSUPPORT user (standard address: *http://<server>.<domain>:5<system number>00/smd*, see Figure 4.27).

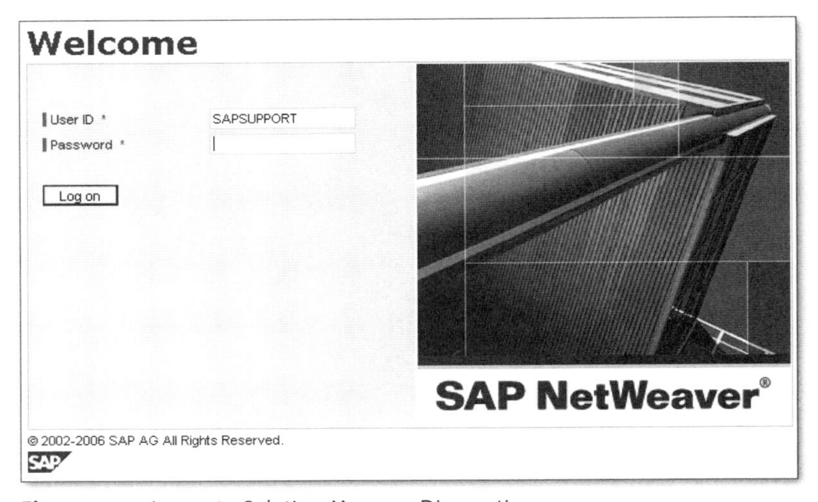

Figure 4.27 Logon to Solution Manager Diagnostics

2. Select the Workload Analysis from the Root Cause Analysis tools.
3. Select your active solution in the landscape selection and define the system role of the system you want to analyze.
4. You can then select the system from the updated list to the right of the selection. If your system is not listed, check another system role or check to see if the system has been implemented in Solution Manager Diagnostics.
5. When you have selected your system, you can open the End-to-End Workload Analysis in the right main window in the navigation bar (see Figure 4.28).
6. The Enterprise Portal tab displays detailed information on the system.

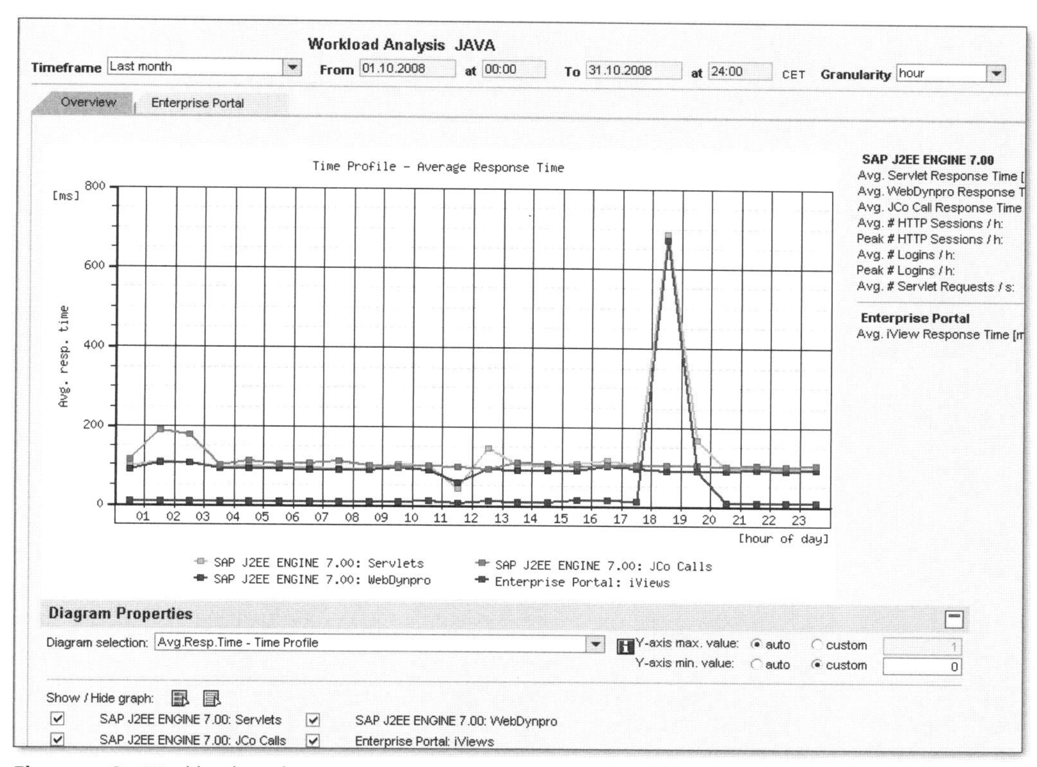

Figure 4.28 Workload Analysis, Enterprise Portal PSI Overview

The Workload Analysis tool in Solution Manager Diagnostics does not provide alert methods, and you cannot define threshold values in the standard views. For more information on the use of these tools, refer to SAP Press Essentials 41, *Performing End-to-End Root Cause Analysis Using SAP Solution Manager*, by Michael Klöffer and Marc Thier (SAP PRESS, 2008). It discusses the use and possible interpretations of information using an example scenario.

4.9 Setting Up Manual System Monitoring

In addition to setting up system monitoring, which focuses on active, automatic monitoring of certain monitoring objects, you can also set up manual system monitoring or system administration using another service in SAP Solution Manager. That means you can define administrative tasks that have to be implemented daily, weekly, monthly, or as needed in the system. For some of these tasks, monitoring objects can be defined in SAP Solution Manager. Outstanding tasks are then displayed in the graphical solution landscape. Implement the setup as follows:

1. Begin in your solution landscape.
2. Select Operations Setup in the left-hand pane.
3. Follow the OPERATIONS SETUP • SYSTEM ADMINISTRATION • CENTRAL SYSTEM ADMINISTRATION <SID> menu path. You are now in the system monitoring setup (see Figure 4.29).

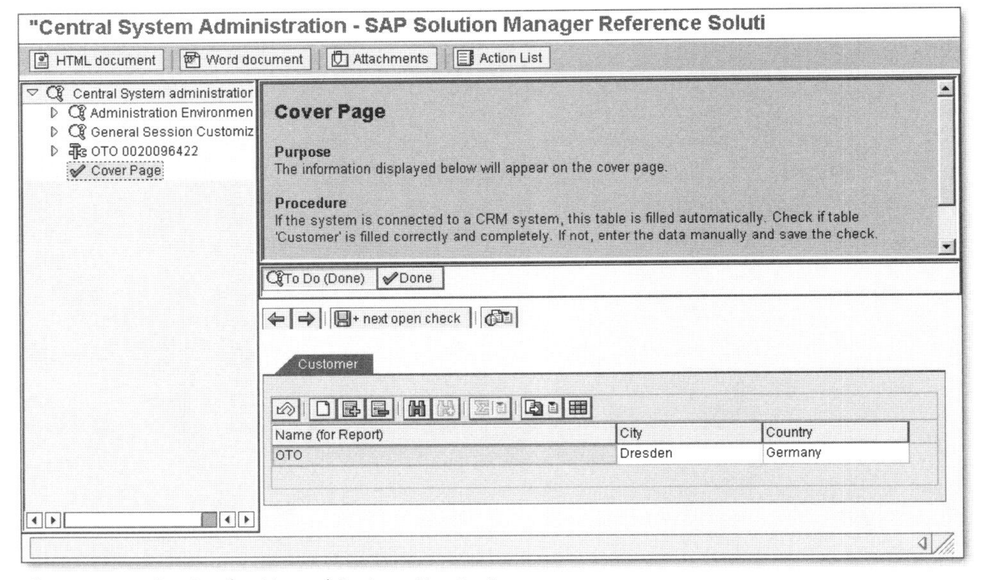

Figure 4.29 Service for Manual System Monitoring

4. Follow the menu path CENTRAL SYSTEM ADMINISTRATION • ADMINISTRATION ENVIRONMENT • CHOOSE ADMINISTRATION AND MONITORING WORKAREA to select which view variant you want to have on the system tasks. Table 4.7 lists the available views.

View	Description
ENTIRE	The system displays all open and completed tasks.
TASK WORKLIST	The system displays all open tasks regardless of their frequency.

Table 4.7 Standard Views of the Task List

View	Description
DAILY OPEN	The system displays all open tasks that are performed daily.
WEEKLY OPEN	The system displays all open tasks that are performed weekly.
MONTHLY OPEN	The system displays all open tasks that are performed monthly.
YEARLY OPEN	The system displays all open tasks that are performed yearly.
PERFORMED TASKS	The system displays all performed tasks regardless of their planned frequency.
SCHEDULED OPEN TASKS	The system displays all scheduled open tasks.
SCHEDULED PERFORMED TASKS	The system displays all scheduled performed tasks.

Table 4.7 Standard Views of the Task List (Cont.)

5. Save your entries.
6. You can modify the view variants via the CENTRAL SYSTEM ADMINISTRATION • TASKS VIEW MASTER menu path. For example, you can just display all open system tasks for this month in a view variant.
7. Save your entries.
8. The report content enables you to create customer-specific reports. To do this, select Report Content. In the right part of the screen, navigate to the Define Content for Task Log History tab to create new report content. Decide whether you want to include tasks with comments in the report. In the Task Logs from Date and Task Logs until Date columns, you can specify the time period for the report output of the tasks. When you have saved your entries, the data is updated to the table for the task log history. The Task Log History tab provides an overview of all of the entries. In the report, these entries are displayed in the same sequence and with the same sorting. To view the task log history as an HTML document, click on the Tasks Log History button.
9. Save your entries.

In the next step, define which system tasks have to be executed at what point in each system.

1. To do this, follow the CENTRAL SYSTEM ADMINISTRATION • <SYSTEM ID INSTALLATION NUMBER> menu path. There are five tabs on the right-hand side of the screen:
   - System Type — Select the system type (production system, quality assurance system, development system, demo system).
   - Involved Component — Select the relevant SAP component for this system. Additional system tasks must be set for the component.
   - Defining User Task Area/Defining User Task Groups/Assigning User Task — In the next three tabs, you can define user-specific or customer-specific tasks. You can assign the tasks in groups or as individual tasks to users.
2. Save your entries.

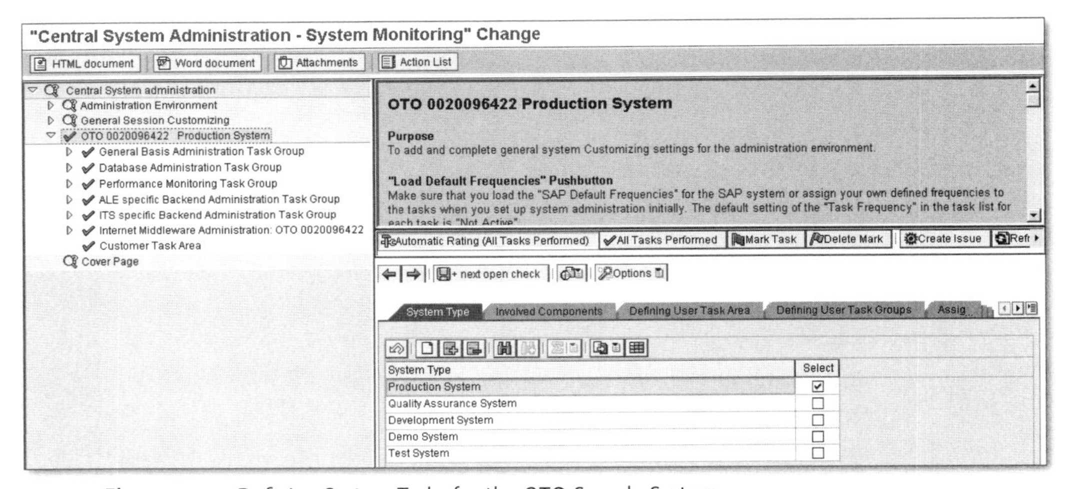

Figure 4.30 Defining System Tasks for the OTO Sample System

Depending on the components selected, you will receive a range of subchecks under <System ID Installation Number>. In our example, these are the following sub-checks for the OTO system (see Figure 4.30):

- General Basis Administration Task Group
- Database Administration Task Group
- Performance Monitoring Task Group
- ALE-specific Backend Administration Task Group

- ITS-specific Backend Administration Task Group
- Internet Middleware Administration: OTO 0020096422
- Customer Task Area

For each of these checks a range of further subchecks is offered. Here, you can select which tasks should be included in your system administration (see Figure 4.31).

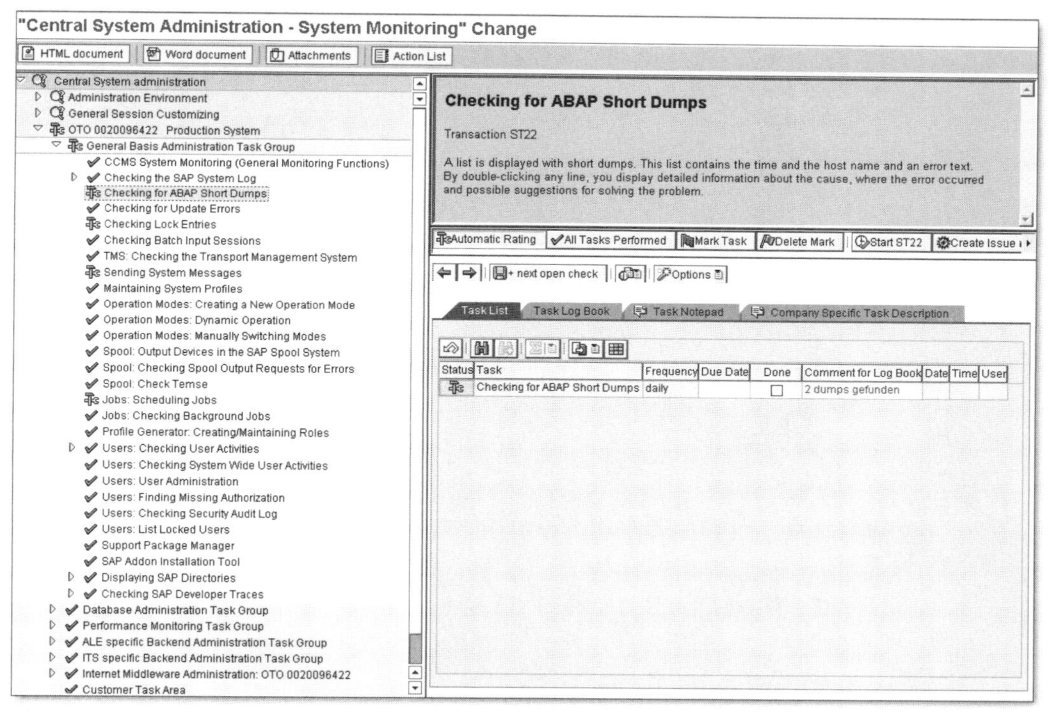

Figure 4.31 Selecting System Tasks for the Selected System

Then, set up system monitoring:

1. Proceed through each individual check step by step and see if this task must be executed in your system monitoring. On the right-hand side of the screen there are four tabs per system task:
   - Task List
     Select the frequency (daily, weekly, monthly, yearly, or not active) of the monitoring activity. You will use the DONE and COMMENT FOR LOG BOOK

columns in the monitoring process. Here, in the case of an alert, you can enter information on the alert and measures you have implemented to resolve the problem. However, for the implementation of central system monitoring this information and the troubleshooting measures are of no relevance.

- Task Log Book
  This task logs which user carried out which system task and when.
- Additional Log Book Comments
  Whoever executed the task can store additional comments on monitoring here. If, for example, an escalation has to be started, this can be logged at this point.
- Company Specific Task Description
  In this tab you can set troubleshooting procedures, escalation procedures, responsibilities, and so on.

2. Save your entries.

After setting up central system monitoring, you will see the symbol instead of a green rating for each task you have defined. It means that a task was defined at this point. You will also find this symbol later in the graphical display of the system monitoring.

Graphical Display of the Central System Administration

After setting up the central administration you can view the result in a graphical overview. The HTML graphic makes the system the administrative tasks are stored in easily recognizable. The system tasks are displayed according to the frequency of the monitoring.

1. Begin in the active solution in SAP Solution Manager.
2. Select Operations.
3. Follow the Solution Monitoring • System Monitoring/Administration menu path. You are now in the graphical overview display for system monitoring and administration. The system displays the status for the manual and automatic monitoring in a mode. If a system is defined for a task list, this is indicated by the clipboard symbol.
4. Select the corresponding symbol in each system. A new dialog opens (see Figure 4.32) that defines the tasks for each system.

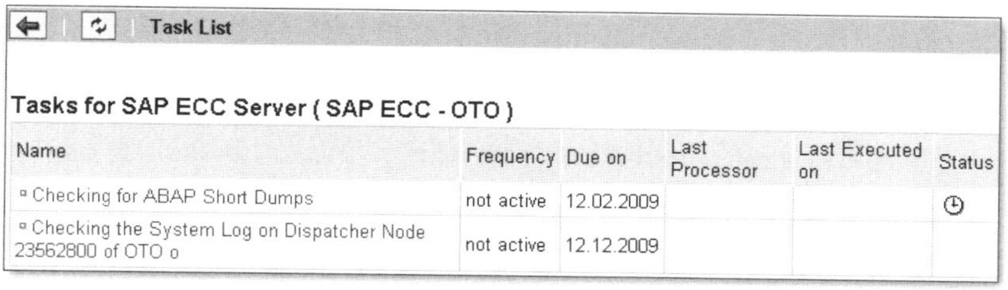

Task List

Tasks for SAP ECC Server (SAP ECC - OTO)

Name	Frequency	Due on	Last Processor	Last Executed on	Status
Checking for ABAP Short Dumps	not active	12.02.2009			
Checking the System Log on Dispatcher Node 23562800 of OTO o	not active	12.12.2009			

Figure 4.32 System Tasks for the ECC System OTO

5. Select a task. You are now in the central system administration service. Here you have the option to go directly into the monitored system to execute the system task. Upon completing the task, confirm this and, if necessary, write a comment into the log book.
6. Save your entries. The symbol is replaced by a green rating. The task disappears from the task list of the graphical overview until the next necessary monitoring activity.

4.10 Autoreaction Methods

Monitoring a system landscape means that the system administrator needs to receive prompt notification of any problems that have occurred. Autoreaction methods such as service tickets, email notifications, short message service (SMS), fax, or pager are very helpful.

The method by which the system administrator receives information on a problem that has occurred depends on what influence the monitored object has on the running system operation. If, for example, a system breaks down, it is recommended to notify the system administrator both through the monitoring team and an autoreaction method.

In the SAP Solution Manager, system autoreaction methods are defined via the CCMS monitoring architecture. Since SAP Basis Release 4.0, the CCMS monitoring architecture gives you the option to define autoreaction methods, which are automatically executed in the case of an alert.

Since SAP Basis Release 7.0, the predefined autoreaction methods, Serv_Desk_Mess_on_Alert and CCMS_OnAlert_Email_V2, are supplied. These methods react to alerts themselves in the background and send the ticket to the Service Desk or a notification via email, fax, SMS, or pager to a recipient or recipient list.

Since SAP Basis Release 6.10, central autoreaction methods can be defined in central monitoring. The autoreaction methods are then configured in the system in which the central monitoring is executed. Section 4.11, Central Autoreaction Methods, provides an example for the implementation of a central email autoreaction method.

This section describes the technical implementation for the email autoreaction methods. That means the prerequisites and functionalities described here are only considered in connection with setting up email traffic for Toys Inc. in an SAP Solution Manager 7.0 system. If you need information on the technical setup for sending information via SMS, fax, or pager, you can get this information from the SAP library (*http://help.sap.com*).

At Toys Inc., the central email autoreaction method is implemented for the OTO, TEC, PSI, PBI and WAMA production system in the SAP Solution Manager system.

The process of automatically creating service tickets in the Service Desk is identical to the email method. If an incident (error) occurs, the system generates on the basis of the error text a ticket, which is sent to the component in the Service Desk that is defined for the method. The Service Desk enables you to create an alert system as defined in IT Infrastructure Library (ITIL). If the ticket is not processed within a defined period of time, it can automatically trigger an escalation.

SAP Press Essentials 46, *SAP Solution Manager Service Desk – Functionality and Implementation*, by Matthias Friedrich and Torsten Sternberg (Galileo Press 2008) describes the implementation and process in the Service Desk in more detail.

4.10.1 SAPconnect

SAPconnect provides a standardized, external communication interface for that supports communication by telecommunication services, such as fax, pager, Internet, and X400, and communication with printers and other SAP systems. It facilitates the connection of external communication components to the SAP system.

There are two ways to link SAPconnect to an SAP system:

- **SAPconnect with RFC**
  SAP's technology from Releases 3.1 to 6.x allows for the connection of various gateways via RFC. These gateways transfer emails between the SAP system and

a specified email server. That means you execute the actual email transfer via SMTP (Internet email protocol) to or from remote participants. For example, email gateways can be the SAP Internet email gateway, SAP Exchange Connector, and also non-SAP products from partner enterprises.

- **SAPconnect with SMTP**
  Using SAP Technology Release 6.10, the SAP system kernel directly supports SMTP. This means that no further components are necessary to send or receive emails from the SAP system to each SMTP-compatible email server. This type of connection is described in the following section.

4.10.2 Setting the Email Autoreaction Method via SMTP in SAP Solution Manager 7.0

The following steps to set up the email autoreaction method through SMTP are described on the basis of SAP NetWeaver 2004s. Furthermore, the setup refers to outgoing emails only. Please note that in other SAP releases deviations in the configuration can occur.

To use the SMTP functionality, the profile must be compatible with SAP NetWeaver 2004s. Set the following profile parameters for SMTP. The <*> placeholder stands for a digit so that the parameters can be numbered consecutively, beginning with 0.

Maintain the parameter

```
icm/server_port_<*> = PROT=SMTP,PORT=<port>
```

in the SAP Solution Manager system. This opens a TCP/IP port to receive emails through the SMTP plug-in. If you don't want to receive any emails, set the port to 0.

A further parameter is

```
is/SMTP/virt_host_<*> = <host>:<port>,<port>,...;.
```

Here, a "virtual host" is defined for the receipt of emails. This parameter is only necessary if several clients are to receive incoming emails. If emails are only received and processed in clients, this parameter is not necessary. This is only mentioned here for the sake of completeness — it is not relevant for the configuration in our Toys Inc. example.

The SAPconnect settings must be set up in the client that sends or receives emails. Here, you define, for example, which email server and port is used to send emails from the system:

1. Call Transaction SCOT. Follow the View • System Status menu path. The SMTP node can be found under the INT (Internet) element.

   Each client contains only one SMTP node. It is automatically created by the system and cannot be deleted.

2. Double-clicking on the SMTP node takes you to the configuration screen (see Figure 4.33).

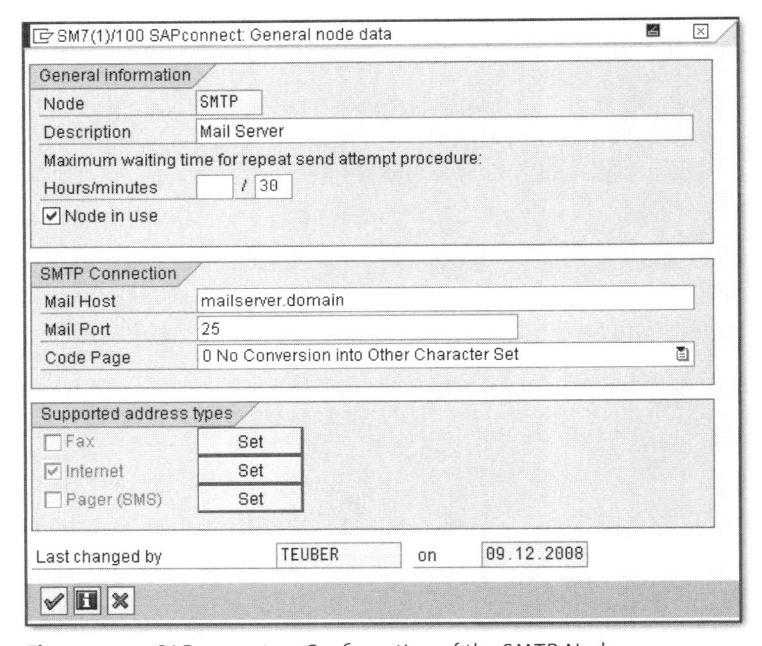

Figure 4.33 SAPconnect — Configuration of the SMTP Node

3. Configure the SMTP node. In the Hours/minutes field, define which time interval the connection must be re-established in for the SMTP nodes if a temporary connection problem occurs.
4. Select the Node in use field.
5. Enter the email server in the Mail Host field and the corresponding port number in the Mail Port field.

6. Click the Internet field and click on the corresponding Set button. A new dialog opens.
7. Enter the address area of the recipient addresses that are to be reached via this node. For example, "*" (asterisk) if all emails are to be sent through the SMTP node.
8. In Output Formats for SAP Documents, using the settings available in Figure 4.34 is recommended.

Output Formats for SAP Documents	
SAPscript/Smart Forms	PDF
ABAP List	HTM
Business Object/Link	TXT
RAW Text	TXT

Figure 4.34 Output Formats for SAP Documents

Emails sent from an SAP system are placed in a queue. The SAPconnect send job periodically checks to see if new emails are in the queue, and, if necessary, sends them. This job is scheduled in the SAP Solution Manager system by SAPconnect administration:

1. Call Transaction SCOT. Follow the View • Jobs menu path. Here, you can check if a send job is scheduled in SAPconnect. If you are not sure, you can also check Transaction SM37 (Simple Job Selection) to see if a job has already been scheduled in the RSCONN01 program.
2. Follow the menu path Job • Create. A dialog opens.
3. Enter a name for the job here.
4. Confirm the entry with the ↵ key or with the green check. A new dialog opens.
5. Select the SAP&CONNECTINT variant (see Figure 4.35).
6. Click on the Schedule button. A new dialog opens.
7. In this dialog, click the Periodic Scheduling button.
8. Set the time interval in which the job is started, for example, every five minutes, and confirm your entry with the Create button or the ↵ key.
9. Follow the GoTo • Display Scheduling menu path or click the Display Scheduling button to see if the job has been successfully created.

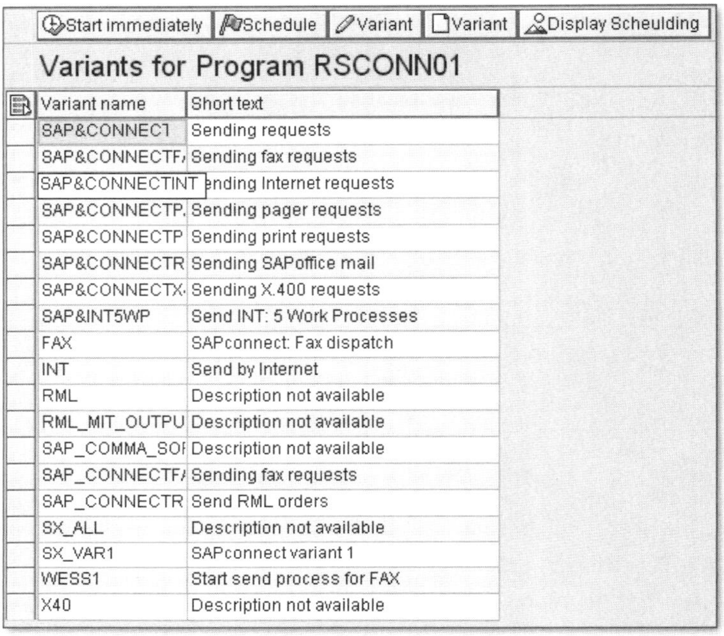

Start immediately | Schedule | Variant | Variant | Display Scheulding

Variants for Program RSCONN01

Variant name	Short text
SAP&CONNECT	Sending requests
SAP&CONNECTF/	Sending fax requests
SAP&CONNECTINT	ending Internet requests
SAP&CONNECTP.	Sending pager requests
SAP&CONNECTP	Sending print requests
SAP&CONNECTR	Sending SAPoffice mail
SAP&CONNECTX·	Sending X.400 requests
SAP&INT5WP	Send INT: 5 Work Processes
FAX	SAPconnect: Fax dispatch
INT	Send by Internet
RML	Description not available
RML_MIT_OUTPU	Description not available
SAP_COMMA_SOI	Description not available
SAP_CONNECTF/	Sending fax requests
SAP_CONNECTR	Send RML orders
SX_ALL	Description not available
SX_VAR1	SAPconnect variant 1
WESS1	Start send process for FAX
X40	Description not available

Figure 4.35 Creating an SAPconnect Send Job — Scheduling Variant for the Send Process

4.11 Central Autoreaction Methods

You can define central autoreaction methods within the scope of central monitoring of SAP components in the CCMS monitoring architecture. The autoreaction methods are not configured and started in the system the alert appears in, but in the central monitoring system, which is SAP Solution Manager in our example. This means that work for setting up and changing autoreaction methods is only required at one point.

For central monitoring, installing the SAPCCM4X agent is required for each system that is monitored and connected to the central system.

SAP systems with Basis Release 3.1 (Release 3.1 requires the SAPCM3X agent) and systems that are centrally connected to SAPCCMSR agents are automatically part of the central monitoring system. Therefore, the autoreaction methods are always started centrally.

4.11.1 Setting Up the Central Autoreaction Method (Using the Email Method as an Example)

The configuration of the central autoreaction method is carried out in the SAP Solution Manager system.

1. Call Transaction RZ21. Follow the TECHNICAL INFRASTRUCTURE • CONFIGURE CENTRAL SYSTEM • ASSIGN CENTRAL AUTOREACTIONS menu path. This takes you to the Manage Central Autoreactions screen (see Figure 4.36).

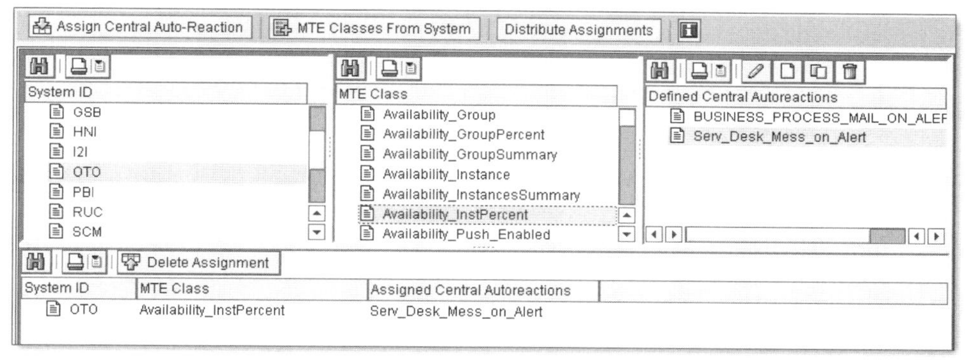

Figure 4.36 Central Autoreactions — Management

The screen is split into four areas. In the upper left-hand System ID area you can see the systems that are connected to the central monitoring system. In the central area there is a selection of MTE classes. On the right-hand side you can see the central autoreaction(s), which you define by assigning systems to the relevant MTE class. In the bottom area you get an overview of the assignments already stored.

2. Define a central autoreaction method. You can do this either through the DEFINE CENTRAL AUTOREACTION menu path or through the Defined Central Autoreactions pane and clicking the Create button. A new dialog opens.

3. Enter your preferred method name into the field next to the Create button. Then, click the Create button.

   Alternatively, you can also execute an existing autoreaction method centrally. To do this, enter the existing method into the entry field next to the Create With Template button and then click this button. The new Monitoring: Methods dialog opens.

4. Enter the corresponding method settings. Note the following settings in the respective tabs:
   - **Execution**
     Enter the report or the function module to be executed. If you like you can use the SALO_EMAIL_IN_CASE_OF_ALERT_V2 function module provided by SAP.
   - **Control**
     Select Only in Central System, trigger by CCMS agents.
   - **Parameters**
     Transfer the parameters according to their values. Figure 4.37 provides an overview of all of the possible parameters and the corresponding value descriptions.
   - **Release**
     Mark the Autoreaction Method field.
5. Save your entries.

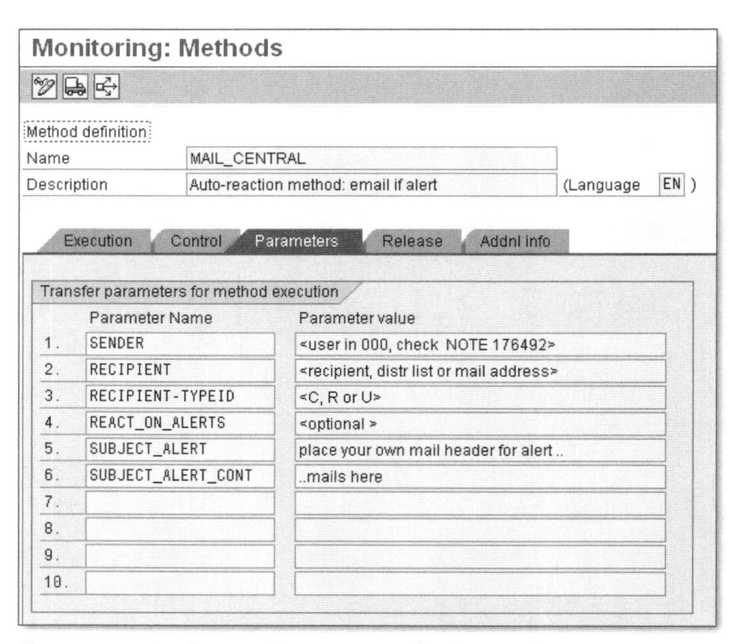

Figure 4.37 Configuring the Parameters for the Email CEN Autoreaction Method

4.11.2 Assigning the Central Autoreaction Method

Proceed as follows to assign the central autoreaction method to the monitored systems:

1. Call Transaction RZ21. Follow the TECHNICAL INFRASTRUCTURE • CONFIGURE CENTRAL SYSTEM • ASSIGN CENTRAL AUTOREACTIONS menu path. This brings you to the Manage Central Autoreactions dialog screen.
2. Select the systems in the System ID area that you want to include in the central autoreaction methods and the MTE class you want to include from the MTE Class area.
   You can select several objects at once by keeping the Ctrl key pressed while selecting the objects.
3. Select the autoreaction method in the Defined Central Autoreactions area that you want to assign to the selected classes and the selected systems.
4. Click on the Assign Central Autoreactions button. In the bottom area you will see the corresponding assignment.

Carry out the steps until you have assigned all of the autoreaction methods to the corresponding systems and the desired MTE class.

4.11.3 Activating Central System Dispatching

Once you have defined and assigned the autoreaction methods, you can activate the central system dispatching.

In Transaction RZ21, Follow the TECHNICAL INFRASTRUCTURE • CONFIGURE CENTRAL SYSTEM • ACTIVATE CENTRAL SYSTEM DISPATCHING menu path.

Ensure that you start the central autoreaction methods under the user name for the client that was activated by the central method dispatcher. If you use the automatic alert notification, the client is crucial. After activation, ensure you are in the client emails are sent from.

4.11.4 Parameter Maintenance of the Email Autoreaction Method

Autoreaction methods, such as emails, can be assigned to an MTE class. If an alarm is triggered for the MTE according to its values, the SAP system automatically sends an email to the specified recipient. Three important pieces of information are necessary for this:

- **Sender**
  The sender is an SAP user name in whose name the email is sent. This user must be available in Client 000. An email address must be assigned to this user.
- **Recipient**
  The recipient can be an Internet address or a mailing list, for example.
- **ID Sender type (Address type)**
  The sender or address type is dependent on the sender. The sender determines the method of communication. If you send an email to an Internet address, the corresponding address type is "U," for example. Possible recipient types with the related address type are listed in Table 4.8.

Recipient Type	Sample Entry	Indicator
Name	Anna Meyer	
SAP user ID	Meyera	B
External address	Frank Miller	A
Personal distribution list	Favorite colleagues	P
Group distribution list	Archiving project	C
Fax number	DE 08912345678 (`<country_key fax_number>`)	F
Internet address	anna.meyer@our_enterprise.com	U
Organizational object	Purchasing (organizational unit)	H
Business object	Office folder	J
Remote SAP name	C11:000:meyer (`<system_name:client:name>`)	R
X.400 address	g=anna;s=meyer; o=c11;ou1=m000; p=enterprise;a=dbp; c=de	X
LDAP address	C=de/o=c11/ou=m000/cn=...	D

Table 4.8 Recipient Types with Address Type

- **Subject**
  You can freely define the subject using 140 characters. You can use placeholders to have the system create individual subject lines for the messages. Table 4.9 illustrates which placeholders you can use in the subject line and their meaning.

Placeholder	Description
$SID	System in which the alert occurred
$NODENAME	Complete name of the monitoring node in which the alert occurred (context, object, attribute)
$SEGMENT	Segment name of the monitoring node (= $INSTANCE)
$INSTANCE	Segment name of the monitoring node (= $SEGMENT)
$CONTEXT	Context name of the monitoring node
$OBJECT	Object name of the monitoring node
$ATTRIBUTE	Attribute name of the monitoring node

Table 4.9 Placeholders for the Subject Design of the Email Autoreaction Method

4.11.5 Monitoring the External Transmission Processes

Transmission processes that come from the central monitoring system can be checked in the Administration of external transmissions monitor. According to a defined time frame, which you specify, you can display all transmission processes as follows:

1. Call Transaction SOST. This takes you to the Transmission Requests monitor (see Figure 4.38).

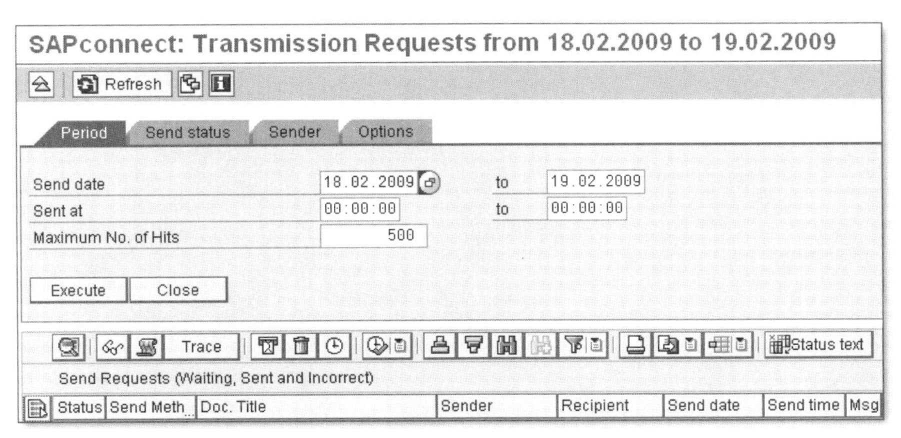

Figure 4.38 Overview of External Transmissions

2. Define the time range in the Send date and Sent time fields for when you want to see the transmission processes.

3. In the Send Status tab, select which transmission status you want to display. You can choose Incorrect, Waiting, Sent, or Transmitted.
4. In the Sender tab, you can restrict the list to a specific user.

Click on the Refresh button or press the F5 key. The analysis of the transmissions is now adapted to the new requirements.

5 IT Performance Reporting

Today, service level agreements (SLAs) are worked out between information technology (IT) and the users to ensure a smooth process flow for the user's department. These agreements describe the user's expectations, for example, for system performance and system availability, and also define parameters for checking their compliance. These parameters can be output in reports.

In many enterprises, reporting has been available for management in the form of business key figures, such as sales, profit, employee workload, business-specific key figures, and so on, for many decades. With the implementation of system-controlled business processes you can integrate additional parameters with reporting, including technical key figures such as system availability, system performance, etc. The more complex the system landscape, the more effort it takes to map and promptly report technical parameters reasonably and correctly.

With SAP Solution Manager you can map and evaluate system information (for example, performance data). You can use IT performance reporting, which is based on information from SAP NetWeaver Business Warehouse (BW), to have the system display monitoring information and statistical data on the performance and use over a certain period of time. You can aggregate this data according to your requirements or evaluate it in detail. IT Reporting Suite already provides a collection of preconfigured reports.

Toys Inc. also decided to implement an extension in IT reporting to call individual information about the system landscape's development in addition to the standard service level report from SAP Solution Manager, which is created for management from the EarlyWatch Alert (EWA) data on a weekly basis.

This chapter describes how you can set up and use IT performance reporting that is based on SAP NetWeaver BW. A step-by-step example describes how you activate the BW system in your SAP Solution Manager system and use it for IT performance reporting. All of the steps can also be implemented in a dedicated BW server. In describing the steps for activating a BW system for IT performance reporting, it is assumed that no BW activation has been performed.

5.1 Prerequisites for IT Performance Reporting

Different source information is used for IT performance reporting. Information from the Computing Center Management System (CCMS), performance statistics, and performance data from the end-to-end scenario (Wily Enterprise Manager data) are stored in BW for performance reportings. To ensure compatibility between the different components, it is important that you install the following components in your SAP Solution Manager production system (see Table 5.1).

Component	Package Names
BW Content	BW_CONT_7.03
SAP Solution Manager	ST
Business Process Management (BPM) information	ST-SER
Diagnostics information	ST-A/PI, ST-PI

Table 5.1 Components for IT Performance Reporting

5.2 Technical Setup of the BW System on SAP Solution Manager

To use the BW system in SAP Solution Manager you first have to set up the configuration. The following sections describe how you can activate the BW system in SAP Solution Manager for IT performance reporting.

5.2.1 Setting Up BW Clients

A BW system has specific requirements for the use of SAP system resources. These deviate from the usual dialog requirements of the Solution Manager production system. To meet the requirements of the Solution Manager production client and the BW system, it is recommended to operate the BW system on a separate client.

There are different options available for using the BW system:

- You can operate your BW system in your Solution Manager production client. Note that you must repeat the sizing of SAP Solution Manager to make the necessary adjustments to the hardware. To do this, refer to the Sizing Guide, which is available in the Service Marketplace under the menu path: SAP COMPONENTS • SAP SOLUTION MANAGER 7.0.

- You can use a dedicated BW system on a separate system. Note that you must also establish communication between the BW system and the Solution Manager production system. This is different from the procedure described in this book.
- You can implement BW analyses using a copied client of the SAP Solution Manager system. To do this, you must create a client copy so that you can use BW analyses in this client. The following describes the scenario and the activation of the BW system based on the client copy.
  - Use Transaction SCCL (see Figure 5.1) to create a local client copy (for example, of Client 001) as the source client for the content to be copied.

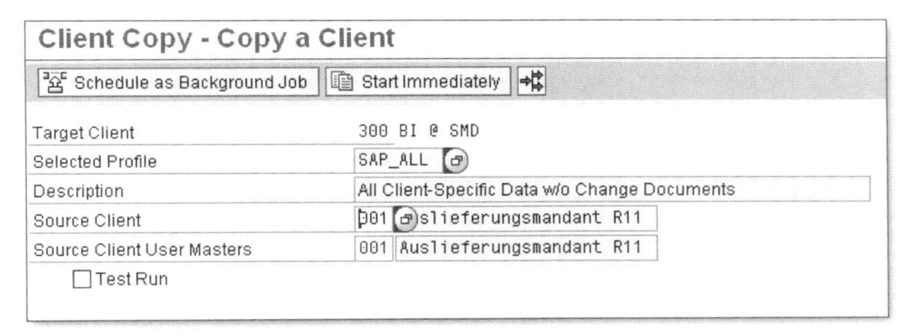

Figure 5.1 Local Client Copy of Delivery Client 001

  - Maintain the BW client as the logical system using Transaction SCC4.
  - In Transaction SE37, select Function Module • Test • Single Test to execute the RS_MANDT_UNIQUE_SET function module.
  - Enter the BW client <CLNT> as the value for the I_MANDT parameter as shown in Figure 5.2.

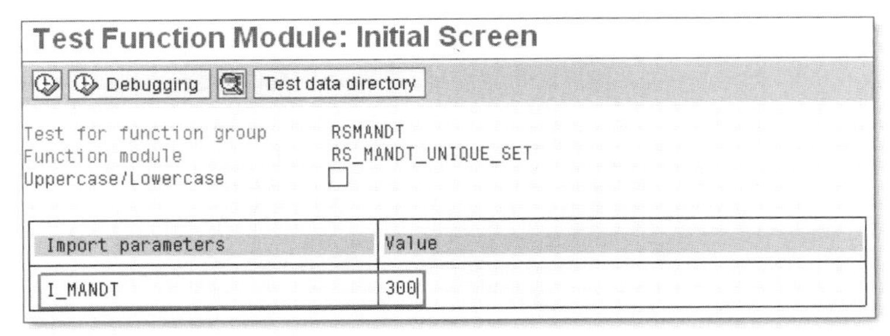

Figure 5.2 Setting the BW Client Using the RS_MANDT_UNIQUE_SET Function Module

  - Select Execute.

5.2.2 Creating Users in the BW System

For communications between your BW client and the Solution Manager production client you must create a background user with the corresponding authorizations and assign the BW client as the BW user for Application Link Enabling (ALE).

The following describes how to create a user in your BW system (for further information, refer to SAP Note 410952):

1. In your BW client, create an ALEREMOTE user of the System User type.
2. Assign the S_BW-WHM_RFC profile to this user.
3. Select Transaction RSA1 (Modeling DW Workbench), and start the replication of the metadata for the BW system.
   - When you call Transaction RSA1 for the first time, the system displays the Replicate Metadata? dialog window in addition to the Activate Replicated Metadata? dialog window (see Figure 5.3). Select Replicate As Well.

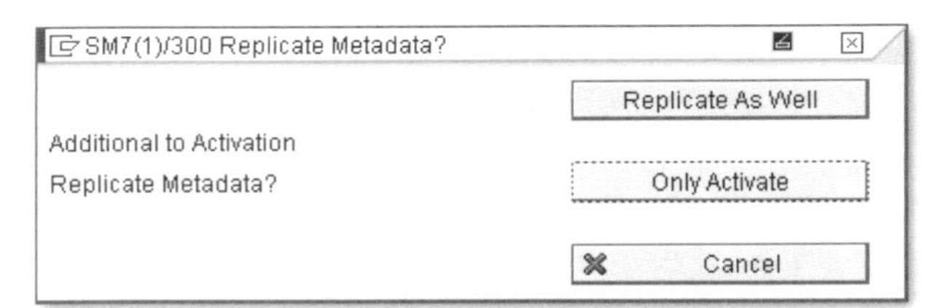

Figure 5.3 Activating the BW Client and Replicating the Content

   - When the system opens another dialog window with the message, DataSource from Source System Unknown. DataSource (OSOA) 80CCMaGGR does not exist in BW system. How do you want to create the object in BW?, select This and following as 3.x DataSource (ISFS) (see Figure 5.4). The system will activate all following DataSources in the old Business Warehouse (BW) Release 3.x format. The new format is not yet supported for performance data and therefore should not be selected.
   - If the dialog windows displays Documentation for Modeling area—Do you want to start the documentation for the Navigation in the modeling view in a separate window?, select Do not show this question again and then Yes.

   (You can also access this function via the menu path: DATA WAREHOUSING WORKBENCH • DOCUMENTATION FOR MODELING.)

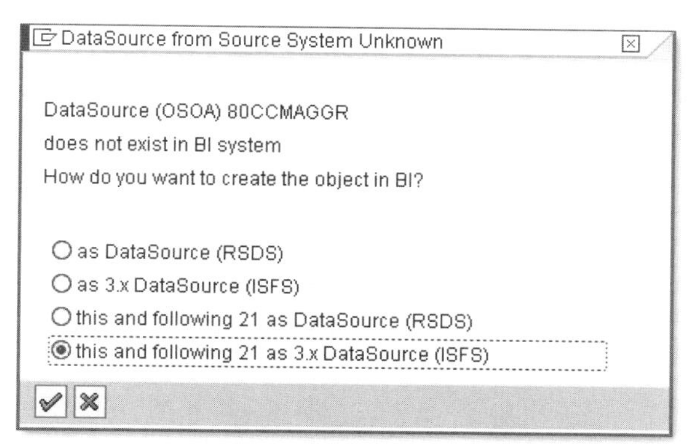

Figure 5.4 Creating Unknown Objects as 3.x Data Sources

4. In the menu, choose Settings • Global Settings.
5. Enter the name of the created background user ALEREMOTE in the BW User for ALE field.
6. Save your entries, and continue the process by connecting the source system.

For more information, see SAP Note 410952.

5.2.3 Connecting the Source System

To access information and data of the BW system from the Solution Manager client, you must establish a communication interface between the source client and the BW client. Here, you can create a Remote Function Call (RFC) connection from the BW client to the client of the source system and from the client of the source system to the BW client.

Proceed as follows:

1. Click the Modeling button in the left area of the screen.
2. Select Source Systems.
3. Highlight the BW folder in the Source Systems column.
4. Right-click Create.

   The system opens a dialog window in which you define the communication via the RFC connection. Proceed in accordance with your prerequisites:

- No RFC connection to the source system exists in the BW system yet:
  In Create New Destination enter the corresponding data for the source system (server, SID, system number).
- An RFC connection to the source system already exists:
  Select the corresponding RFC connection in the Available Destination field.

Note

Even if your Solution Manager production client is the BW client, you must specify a corresponding RFC connection, for example, <SID>CLNT<client>.

5. In Background User in Source System enter the name (for example, ALEREMOTE) and the password for the background user in the source system.

   This background user is automatically created as the system user with the S_BW-WX_RFC profile in the source system and is assigned to the created RFC connection.

6. Specify the password of the background user you created in the BW client in Background User in BW.

Note

If your Solution Manager production client is the BW client, you must specify the ALEREMOTE user for the source system and the BW system and assign the appropriate profiles to this user.

7. Click Continue.
8. Log on to the client of the source system as the administration user.
9. Confirm the dialog window for the user and password.
10. If the system displays a dialog window for replicating the metadata, select Replicate.
11. In the following dialog windows, select this and all following 3.x DataSources (ISFS) as the DataSource.

After you've successfully created the source system in the BW client, the system creates the following RFC connections:

- In the source system: <SID>CLNT<CLNT> with logon user (for example, ALEREMOTE)

- In the BW client: <SID>CLNT<CLNT> with logon user (for example, ALEREMOTE) and <SID>CLNT<CLNT>_DIALOG

5.2.4 Activating the Service for the Business Explorer (BEx) and Setting Up the External Alias for the Service /default_host/sap/bw/BEx

The service for the Business Explorer (BEx) (/default_host/sap/bw/BEx), which controls the call of reports in the BW client, is not active by default and must therefore be activated for the tools, such as IT Reporting Suite. The reports that are provided in IT Reporting Suite, for example, are called in the current session as an HTTP service. To avoid a logon to the calling BW client, you should define the appropriate external alias in the service. It is recommended to define this external alias in the service properties as a mandatory logon; this prevents the system from repeatedly prompting you to logon after you've called a report in the work center of SAP Solution Manager, for example.

The following activities are necessary to call reports from the BW system in the work center without logon:

Use Transaction SICF_INST to execute the report with the technical name, SM_SOLUTION_MONITORING, in the Solution Manager production client (see Figure 5.5).

Figure 5.5 Executing the Report SM_SOLUTION_MONITORING in Transaction SICF_INST

After the report has been run successfully, you should check the activation.

1. Start Transaction SICF and select the SERVICE hierarchy type.
2. Click Execute.
3. In the service tree, go to the /BEx service via the intermediate nodes, /DEFAULT_HOST • /SAP • /BW, and select this service as shown in Figure 5.6.

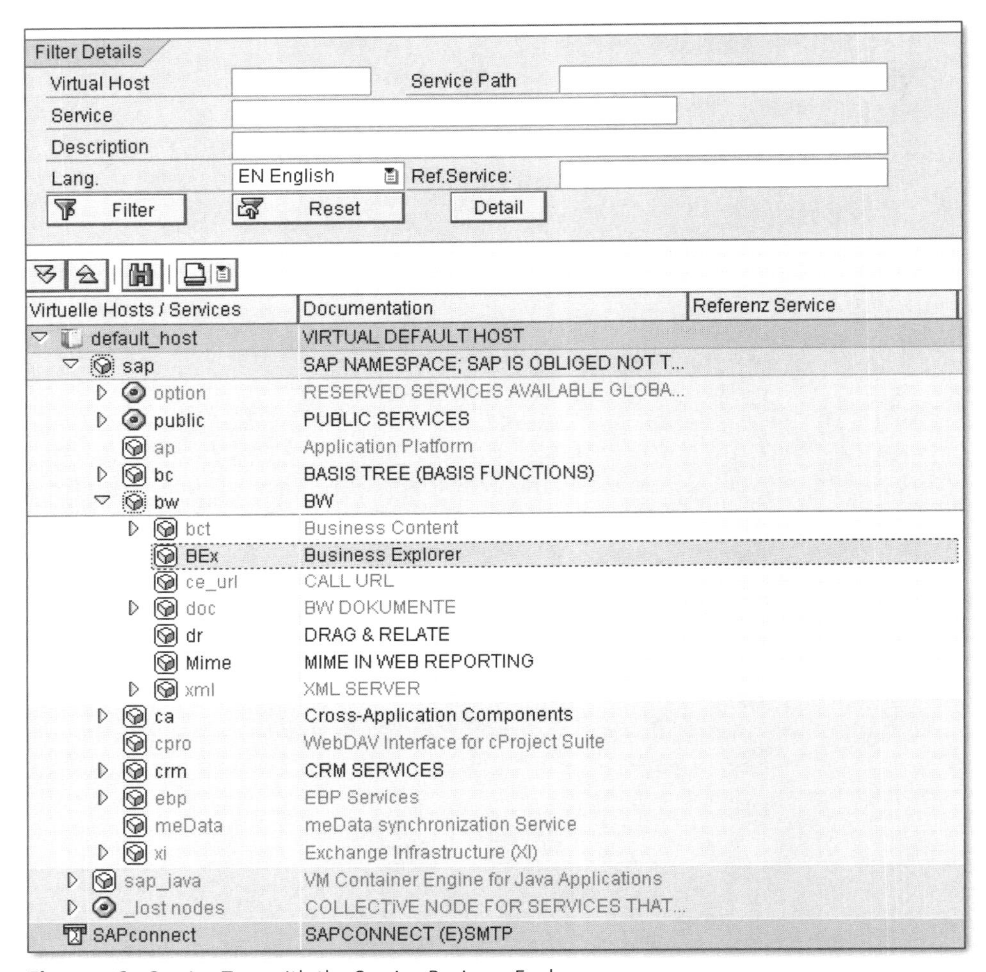

Figure 5.6 Service Tree with the Service Business Explorer

4. In the context menu, select the Test Service entry. A new window opens in the browser.

After you've activated the service, you should create the external alias for the service.

1. In Transaction SICF, select External Aliases as the hierarchy type.
2. Click on Execute.
3. Highlight `default_host` in the display.
4. Select External Alias • Create from the menu. A dialog window opens.
5. Enter /sap/bw/BEx as the name of the external alias.
6. In the Logon Data tab, check the field, Procedure Required with Logon Data.
7. Specify the corresponding BW client and the communication user (from Section 5.2.2, Creating Users in the BW System) as the client. Select ALEREMOTE here.
8. Go to the Target Element tab.
9. Select Default_Host • SAP • BW • BEx.

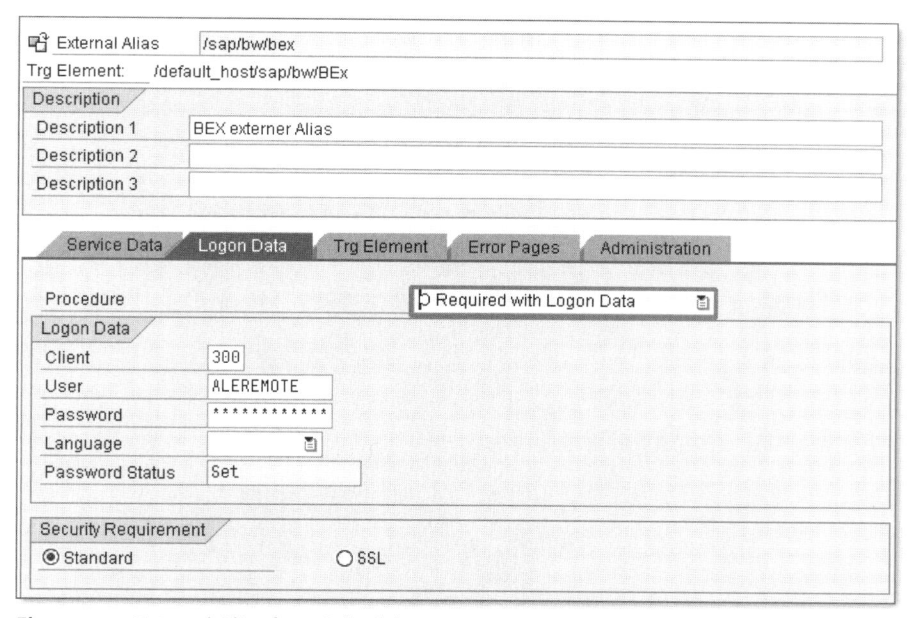

Figure 5.7 External Alias for a Call of the Business Explorer Without Logon

10. Save your entries.

You must click on Cancel to return to the main screen of the external alias.

5.3 Setting Up IT Performance Reporting

5.3.1 Configuring Users for Work Centers

To enable your end users to work with the IT performance reporting in SAP Solution Manager, you must assign the corresponding *System Monitoring* work center to their accounts.

Assign the following authorizations to your user accounts:

- SAP_SMWORK_SYS_MON
- SAP_SMWORK_BASIC

Note that all authorization objects are implemented according to your requirements in the SAP_SMWORK_BASIC role. Only the SAP_SMWORK_BASIC role contains authorizations that are used for executing activities in the work center. All other roles with the SAP_SMWORK* structure serve to visualize individual topic areas in the work center. The topics that the system displays as tabs to the users in the work center (implemented via ABAP Web Dynpros) are based on the roles you select. You can find further information on the work center and its authorizations in the Service Marketplace under the */solutionmanager* quick link. In the Related Topics category, you can find the link to Work Center in SAP Solution Manager.

5.3.2 Activating BW Data Cubes for IT Reporting Suite

To use Reporting Suite you must activate the corresponding service and populate the cubes (0CPH*, 0CCM*) (see Figure 5.8).

To do this, implement the following measures:

1. Use Transaction solman_workcenter to call the work center overview.
2. Navigate to the System Monitoring view and to Setup in the left navigation bar.
3. Select the Configure IT Performance Reporting link from the screen.

   The system checks to see if the setup is possible. This may take some time.

   If the check is successful, the system displays a screen in which you are prompted to continue or cancel.
4. Click Continue.

The system automatically activates and configures the content or allows changes to the existing activation and configuration of the content.

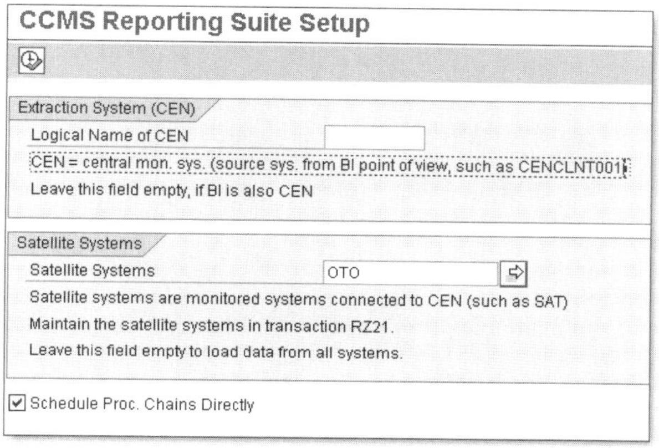

CCMS Reporting Suite Setup
Extraction System (CEN)
Logical Name of CEN
CEN = central mon. sys. (source sys. from BI point of view, such as CENCLNT001)
Leave this field empty, if BI is also CEN
Satellite Systems
Satellite Systems OTO
Satellite systems are monitored systems connected to CEN (such as SAT)
Maintain the satellite systems in transaction RZ21.
Leave this field empty to load data from all systems.
Schedule Proc. Chains Directly

Figure 5.8 IT Reporting Suite Setup

5. When prompted, specify the source system.
6. Run the report.

The activation may take some time. The duration depends on the hardware resources and the activities in the system at the time of the content activation.

5.4 EWA Information in BW Reporting

In addition to the statistics and system monitoring information, you can also use EWA information for BW reporting. This requires some manual activation steps in the BW system to automatically provide content there. The following sections first describe the activation of the data containers based on an EWA data example. By defining the data containers, you ultimately determine the content you can display in your future reports. This is followed by an EWA data example of how you can define and automate the process of data selection, transfer, and display.

5.4.1 Installing DataSources from Business Content

Information that is sent to the BW system must correspond to the data containers of the BW system and adapted, if necessary, to ensure the consistency of information at all times. For IT performance reporting, predefined business contents already exist in which the source and resolution are already defined in the BW system. For the EWA information you have to activate the SAP_BW_Solution_Manager content (see Figure 5.9). Carry out the following steps in the BW client of Solution Manager:

1. Start Transaction RSA6.
2. Under the 0SM_SMG_ROOT node, select the 0SM_SMG node.

   Proceed as follows to search for the node:

   - Click on the Search button.
   - Enter 0SM_SMG*.
3. Select Edit • Select Block from the menu.
4. Click on Activate DataSources.

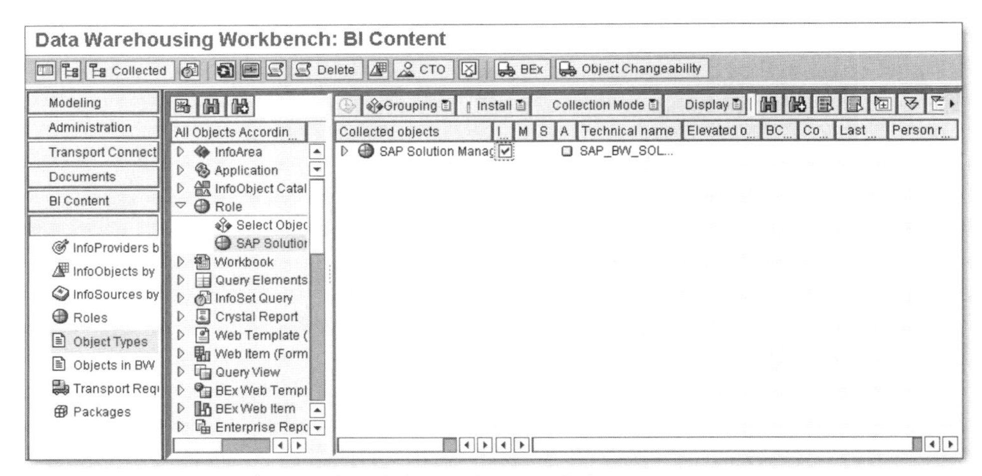

Figure 5.9 Activating the SAP_BW_Solution_Manager Role

After you've activated the DataSources, you must define them via an installation for the source system. This means that the source must be synchronized with the DataSources' containers in such a way that all information intended in the DataSource can be assigned correctly. Perform the following steps for the installation of the BW content:

1. Start Transaction RSOR for the installation of the BW content.
2. Select BW Content • Object Types in the left tree.
3. Select the Role object type.

4. Double-click Select Objects.
5. Copy the `SAP_BW_Solution_Manager` object and transfer the data. In the top right window, the system displays your SAP Solution Manager selection as a grouping.
6. Under Grouping, select the In Dataflow Before and Afterwards option.
7. To install the objects, select INSTALL • INSTALL from the selection menu.

   The installation takes about 15 to 20 minutes. Subsequently, proceed as follows:

8. Follow the menu path: MODELING • INFOPROVIDER • SAP SOLUTION MANAGER 0SM_SMG.
9. Check to see if all business objects are active:
   - InfoCubes
   - DSO objects
   - 3x InfoSources
   - DataSources
   - Update rules
   - Transfer rules
   - InfoPackages

If required, repeat steps 1 to 7 for the business objects that you could not activate or install the first time.

5.4.2 Installing and Activating Process Chains

Process chains automatically perform processes of procurement, automatic filling of content, and aggregating and cleansing of already-expired data. You can automate these processes using process chains that are defined accordingly. They run with a predefined periodicity in the background of Solution Manager. To ensure that the data contained in your reports is always correct and collected within the defined period, you should include the flow of the process chains in monitoring using monitoring tools.

The following describes how you can schedule already-defined process chains. You can also define process chains yourself that automatically carry out the desired processes in the background of the BW system. You can find detailed information on process chains in the book, *SAP Business Intelligence* by Norbert Egger et al. (SAP PRESS 2007).

1. Start Transaction RSA1.
2. Select BW CONTENT • OBJECT TYPES in the left tree.
3. Select the Process Chain object type.
4. Double-click Select Objects.
5. Select all objects in the 0SM_* namespace and confirm the selection.
6. Under Grouping, select the In Dataflow Before and Afterwards option.
7. To carry out the installation, select INSTALL • INSTALL from the selection menu.

Then check the activation of the process chains:

1. Under the SAP Solution Manager node, select Process Chains.
2. Check to see if all of the process chains are active.

Double-click inactive process chains and follow the menu path: PROCESS CHAIN • ACTIVATE.

5.5 Evaluations Using the IT Performance Reporting Suite

After you've implemented all configurations, you can carry out the IT reporting via the *System Monitoring* work center of SAP Solution Manager.

The IT Performance Reporting Suite enables you to create the following evaluations based on the collected information:

- Availability: instance availability
- Performance
  - System load overview
  - Users logged on
  - Server load (CPU, file system)
  - Database load
- Consumption
  - Java session and threads
  - Java garbage collection

You can collect the listed evaluations over different time intervals. In addition, you can preselect the desired systems or system groups to output the information for a specific system (see Figure 5.10).

To start Reporting Suite, proceed as follows:

1. Use Transaction solman_workcenter to call the work center overview.
2. Select the *System Monitoring* work center.
3. Navigate to the Reports area.
4. Select the IT Performance Reporting link.
5. A new window opens in the browser. Select the subject area and the system to be evaluated via the Report menu. You can specify the results via the time intervals.
6. The evaluation is displayed in the lower area of the screen.

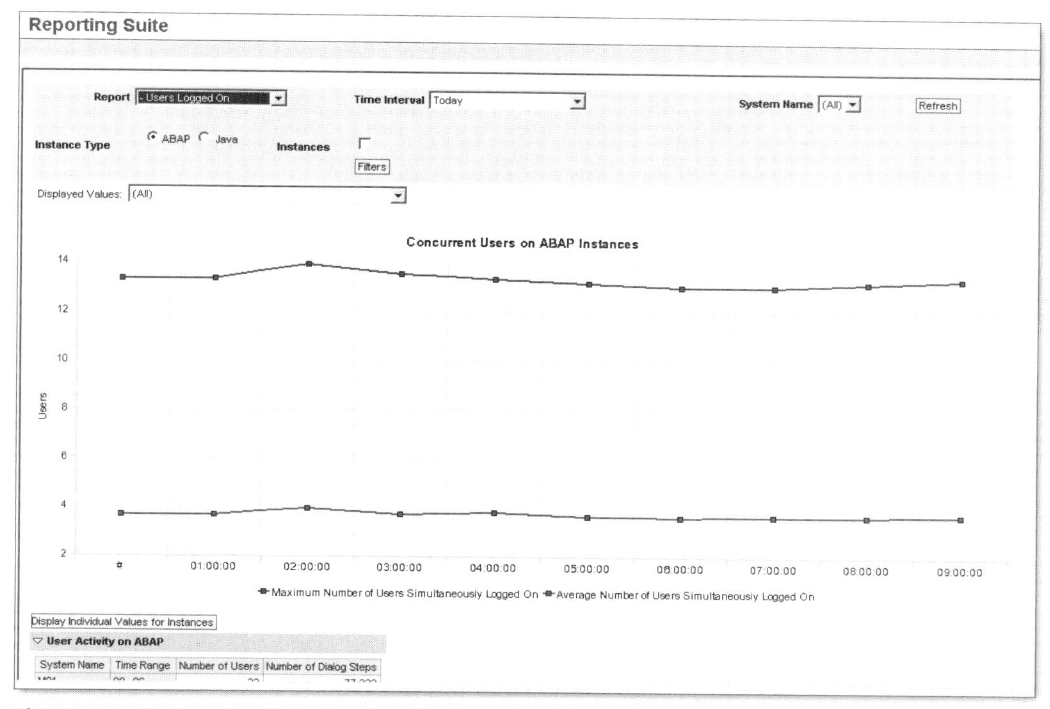

Figure 5.10 IT Reporting Suite Based on the Example of the Evaluation of Users Logged On — Time Interval Yesterday

6 Final Considerations

Throughout the practice sections of this book you have not only implemented a monitoring system in SAP Solution Manager, you have also ventured into the realm of centralized system monitoring. The implementation and configuration of system monitoring in SAP Solution Manager was successfully achieved through precise and meticulous preparation. This involved making a distinction between system monitoring and other functional areas and selecting system components with their monitoring components. You learned what to focus on in the conceptual phase of the project developing a monitoring concept from our example enterprise, Toys Inc. You also learned what activities are necessary to successfully implement the monitoring concept in SAP Solution Manager.

You should not be under the misconception that upon completing the practice examples your work is done. It is now up to you to test the system monitoring solution that has been implemented. By using typical testing examples or scenarios, which you have experienced through the course of your work, you can simulate possible system problems. This means that you should not only test if various monitoring objects set off alarms or autoreaction methods, but you also need to re-create troubleshooting and escalation procedures. In particular, you need to ensure that the processes are harmonious and that they can be easily managed by existing employees. The best process description is not particularly useful if the people responsible are not available or if there isn't sufficient know-how to solve a specific problem.

After a successful test phase and once the central system monitoring is in operation, another phase in the follow-up work begins — the optimization of your system monitoring model. In this context it is advisable to check alarms triggered by individual monitoring objects that have been implemented, according to their threshold value definitions. It is often the case that threshold values have been set too low and therefore an alarm is triggered prematurely by exceeding or running under the value. You can deduce from this that the triggered alarm is not a real critical condition of the system. You should also check to see if sufficient autoreaction methods have been defined for individual monitoring objects. Maybe there are still one or more objects that require an autoreaction method. Or maybe you think that a system component should be integrated into the monitoring system more, even if this did not appear to be the case at the beginning.

As you can see, there is no one monitoring concept that would apply to all system landscapes. It is not only the different information technology (IT) landscapes that make the concept nontransferable, but also the differing views on system monitoring held by individual people. Each person has their own reason why they regard something as being important in system monitoring. This very point is what makes it so important to appoint a person responsible for a project who can bring experience of system monitoring to provide a better insight into the value, or lack thereof, in individual monitoring objects. There are some rules of thumb that you can make use of in system monitoring. But apart from this, each system can be adapted according to individual system conditions.

We hope that this book not only brought home the necessity of a centralized monitoring system, but also highlighted the work involved in introducing system monitoring and the uses that can be made of it.

The Authors

Corina Weidmann holds a degree in Information Management and has worked at SAP SI AG in Dresden, Germany, since 2000. There she gained experience in remote performance analysis for R/3 systems before she specialized in SAP APO and solution monitoring, in particular. At SAP, she provided valuable support for the development of business process monitoring through her own projects using SAP Solution Manager. Today, Corina Weidmann is the managing director of Bautzen IT Consulting GmbH in Dresden, Germany.

Lars Teuber holds a degree in Information Management and worked at SAP SI AG in Dresden, Germany, from 2003 to 2007. While working on projects for national and international customers, he gained experience in system monitoring and performance reporting. Since 2008, he has worked at BIT Consulting GmbH in Dresden, Germany, where he has been able to expand his knowledge of SAP Solution Manager in SAP Solution Manager development projects. He works in system monitoring, performance analysis, and implementation of SAP Solution Manager in projects with regard to both design and implementation.

Index

M

N

O

P

Q

R

S

T

U

W

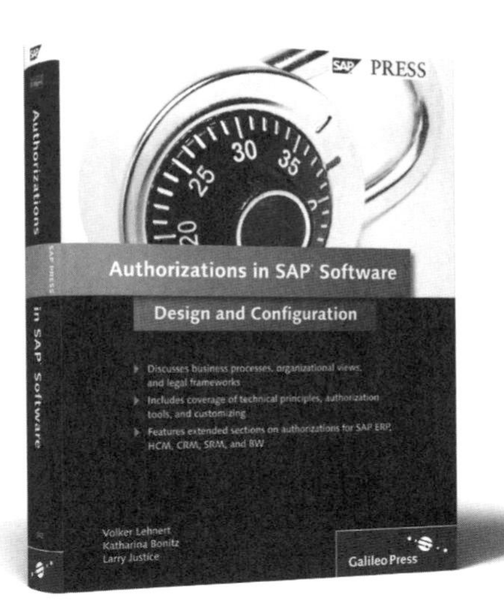
SAP PRESS
Authorizations in SAP Software
Design and Configuration
Galileo Press

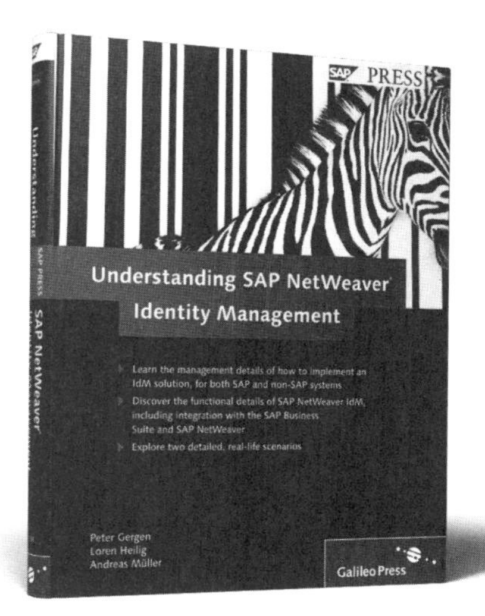
SAP PRESS
Understanding SAP NetWeaver
Identity Management
Peter Gergen
Loren Heilig
Andreas Müller
Galileo Press